职业教育数字化融媒体特色教材

U0647916

AN OVERVIEW OF MICE DESTINATION

会奖目的地概况
（汉英对照）

主　编◎ 柯淑萍
副主编◎ 吴　洁　陈积峰
参　编◎ 陈树平　包文馨　边宇琪　张丽琴

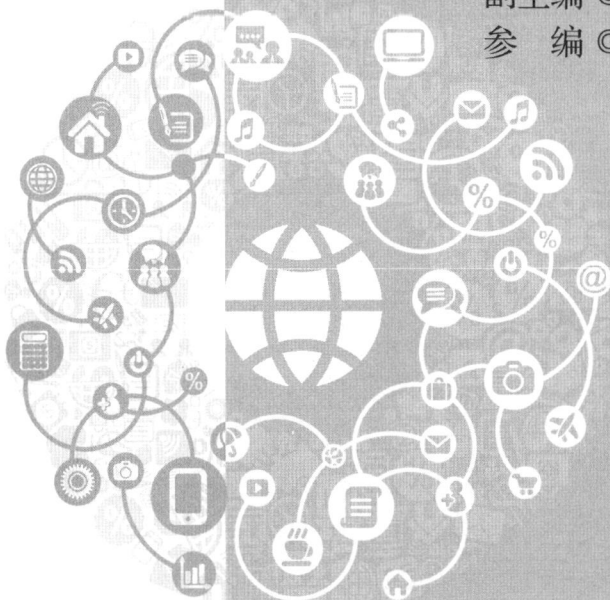

ZHEJIANG UNIVERSITY PRESS
浙江大学出版社

前 言
—————————— F O R E W O R D

　　会奖旅游（MICE）位于高端旅游市场金字塔的塔尖，以规模大、时间长、档次高和利润丰厚为特征。它不仅强调会议或展会本身，更强调给予与会者独特的旅游体验。会奖旅游是一个巨大的市场，对区域经济发展有极大的推动作用。面对广阔的市场前景，如何培养会奖旅游业的专业人才和服务人才是行业关注的热点问题。根据市场调研，目前已有一些高等院校开设了会奖旅游方向的课程，如"会奖英语""会奖目的地概况""会奖策划与营销"等，以期从业者了解会奖旅游业的发展趋势、人才需求特征及职业定位，推动会奖旅游业健康持续发展。遗憾的是，编者搜遍国内整个图书市场，找不到一本相关教材，只能凭借手编资料及会展、旅游相关的教材辅助教学。鉴于此，我们编写了《会奖目的地概况（汉英对照）》新形态教材，以文字及教学视频两种方式呈现国内外 25 个会奖目的地城市，让从业者对会奖目的地城市的概况有直观的了解，对每个会奖目的地城市的不可替代性，比如独特的旅游资源或独特的产业优势，有清晰的判断。本教材以汉英双语的方式编写，视频也是用中英双语的方式呈现，音频全英文，教学视频中包含大量的图片及数据，期待学习者在掌握会奖目的地概况的同时，英语语言能力也有所突破。

　　因为时间紧迫，手头能够收集到的资料有限，教材中的错误与不足在所难免，欢迎各位专家及从业者批评指正。

编 者

2021 年 5 月 20 日于浙江旅游职业学院

目 录

———————— C O N T E N T S

1 会奖旅游业概况
An Overview of MICE Industry

1.1 会奖旅游业概况
An Overview of MICE Industry

　　会奖旅游在国际上简称 MICE，由会议（meeting）、奖励旅游（incentive）、大会（convention/conference）、展览（exhibition/event）4 个部分组成。MICE 服务商利用自身在国际上或行业中的强大号召力举办各种会议和展览活动。奖励旅游则是公司为激励优秀员工、经销商或代理商开展的"非比寻常"的主题旅游，如品尝意大利葡萄酒、体验地中海式的浪漫、领略非洲原生态的动物大迁徙等。全新的思想与理念，造就层出不穷的新玩法。会奖旅游以时间跨度长、参与规模大、产品档次高、利润丰厚为特点，尤其是国际会奖旅游，是一个富有潜力的市场，是高端旅游市场含金量最高的部分。全球每年大约有 350 万人进行会奖旅游活动，为会奖旅游业带来了丰厚的利润。会奖旅游业对区域经济的带动作用巨大。

　　Meeting, Incentive, Convention and Exhibition Tourism is abbreviated as MICE internationally and consists of four parts: meeting, incentive, convention/conference, and exhibition/event. MICE service providers hold various meetings, conventions, and exhibitions with their strong appeal in the world or industry. Incentive tourism is an "extraordinary" theme tourism carried out by companies to motivate outstanding employees, distributors or agents, such as tasting Italian wine, experiencing Mediterranean romance, appreciating original animal migration in Africa. Brand-new ideas and concepts have created endless new entertainments. MICE is characterized by long time span, large scale of participation, high-quality products, and rich profits. International MICE is particularly a potential market and the most valuable part of high-end tourism market. There are about 3.5 million people in the world to participate in MICE activities every year, which has brought MICE huge profits. MICE industry has a great driving effect on the regional economy.

纽约、柏林、巴黎等国际名城利用自身的优势与品牌营销在国际会奖旅游业中快速成长起来，成为会奖旅游业的引领者。世界上任何一个成功的会奖目的地，都有着其他城市不可替代的个性特色。比如，拉斯维加斯博彩业高度发达，柏林被誉为创意艺术家的圣地，奥兰多拥有迪士尼乐园和环球影城，墨尔本传承了百年澳网和传奇赛马，日内瓦聚集了 200 多个重量级的国际组织总部和常设机构，开普敦有无可替代的原生态自然资源。

New York, Berlin, Paris and other international famous cities have made use of their respective advantages and brand marketing to grow rapidly in the international MICE industry, and become the leaders of the industry. Any successful MICE destination in the world has its unique characteristics which cannot be replaced by other cities. For example, Las Vegas's gambling industry is highly developed. Berlin is known as the holy capital of creative artists. Orlando owns Disneyland and Universal Studios. Melbourne inherits Centennial Australian Open and legendary horse racing. Geneva has gathered more than 200 heavyweight international organizations headquarters and permanent institutions. Cape Town has irreplaceable original natural resources.

中国会奖旅游业起步较晚，但经过十多年的发展，已经建立起了自己的行业地位，为下一步向更高、更深、更广阔的方向发展奠定了很好的基础。通过顶层设计、资源整合、会奖旅游市场细分，北京、上海、杭州、成都、西安等国内城市正成为国际青睐的会奖目的地城市。在 2019 年国际大会与会议协会（ICCA）发布的全球会议城市排名中，中国 2019 年国际会议数量排名上升至全球第七位，北京、上海、杭州入围 ICCA 全球城市百强名单。了解国内外会奖目的地城市的概况有助于分析会奖旅游业发展趋势、人才需求特征及从业者职业发展等问题，推进会奖旅游业沿着持续、健康、创新的道路发展。接下来我们将对会奖旅游业的高频词及图标做一个快速浏览。

China's MICE industry started late, but after more than ten years of development, it has established its own industry status, which has laid a good foundation for the next step to a higher, deeper and broader direction. Through top-level design, resource integration and subdivision of MICE market, domestic cities such as Beijing, Shanghai, Hangzhou, Chengdu, Xi'an are becoming international favorite MICE destinations. In the International conference city ranking released by ICCA in 2019, China's number of international conferences in 2019 rose to the seventh in the world, and Beijing, Shanghai, and Hangzhou were shortlisted in ICCA's top 100 cities. It is helpful to analyze the development trend of MICE industry, the characteristics of talent demand, and the career development of practitioners by understanding an overview of domestic and foreign MICE destinations, to promote the sustainable, healthy, and innovative development of MICE industry. Now let's take a quick browse of the high-frequency words and logos of MICE industry.

1.2 相关高频词及图标
Related High-frequency Words and Logos

1.2.1 ICCA

ICCA 是国际会议与会议协会的英文缩写，创建于 1963 年，总部位于阿姆斯特丹，是国际会议最为全球化的组织，目前在全球近 100 个国家或地区拥有超过 1,100 家会员公司和组织机构。ICCA 专注于国际协会会议，ICCA 会员代表来自全球最佳目的地，也是最有经验的专业供应商。国际会议策划者可以依靠 ICCA 平台为他们的所有活动目标寻找一条龙的服务。

ICCA is the abbreviation of International Congress and Convention Association, founded in 1963 and headquartered in Amsterdam. It is the most global organization of international conventions. It currently has more than 1,100 member companies and organizations in nearly 100 countries or regions around the world. ICCA focuses on international association meetings. ICCA member representatives come from the world's best destinations, and they are the most experienced professional suppliers. International conference planners can rely on the ICCA platform to find a one-stop service for all their event goals.

1.2.2 UFI

UFI 是国际展览联盟的简称，原为法文 Union des Foires Internationales 的缩写，是领先的环球协会，代表了世界各地的贸易展览会主办方、展馆运营方、重要的全国性和国际性展览协会，以及精选的展览业服务供应商。UFI 在全球 90 个国家或地区拥有 800 多个会员企业，并有 1,000 多个展览会已经获得了 UFI 认可，为参展商和参会商提供了质量保证。

UFI is the abbreviation of Global Association of the Exhibition Industry, formerly the abbreviation of Union des Foires Internationales in French. It is a leading global association representing trade fair organizers, exhibition hall operators, and important national and international exhibition associations, as well as selected exhibition industry service providers. UFI has more than 800 member enterprises in 90 countries or regions and more than 1,000 exhibitions have been approved by UFI, providing quality assurance for exhibitors and exhibitors.

1.2.3　WTA

世界旅游大奖（简称 WTA）创立于 1993 年，旨在表彰、奖励和庆祝全球旅游业及酒店业有关领域的卓越成就。今天，世界旅游大奖品牌已被全球公认为行业卓越的终极标志，被《华尔街日报》称为旅游行业的"奥斯卡"。

World Travel Awards (WTA) was established in 1993 to acknowledge, reward, and celebrate excellence in the field of the tourism and hospitality industries. Today, the brand of World Travel Awards has been recognized globally as the ultimate symbol of industry excellence, and is called the "Oscar" of the tourism industry by *The Wall Street Journal*.

1.2.4　UNESCO

联合国教育、科学及文化组织简称联合国教科文组织，成立于 1945 年，有 195 个成员，旨在通过教育、科学和文化促进各国各地区合作，为世界和平和安全做出贡献。

United Nations Educational, Scientific and Cultural Organization (UNESCO) was established in 1945 and has 195 members. It aims to promote cooperation among countries or regions through education, science and culture, making contribution to world peace and security.

1.2.5 The World Heritage List

《世界遗产名录》于1976年世界遗产委员会成立时建立，世界遗产委员会隶属于联合国教科文组织。被列入《世界遗产名录》的地方，将成为世界级的名胜，能够得到世界的关注与保护。

"The World Heritage List" was established in 1976 when the World Heritage Committee was established, which is part of UNESCO. Places included in "The World Heritage List" will become world-class scenic spots that can receive the attention and protection of the world.

1.2.6 GaWC

全球化与世界城市研究网络（GaWC）作为城市在全球化过程中的领先智囊团，在国际商务、可持续性、城市政策和物流等相关领域进行了多元化研究。GaWC将入围的世界城市划分为5档12级，最高层次的"全球城市"为a++级。

Globalization and World Cities Study Group and Network (GaWC) operates as the leading thinktank on cities in globalization and has diversified into related subjects on international business, sustainability, urban policy, and logistics. GaWC divides the shortlisted global cities into 5 classes and 12 levels, and the highest "global city" is a＋＋.

1.2.7 ITB

ITB 是国际旅游交易会的简称。ITB Berlin 是全球规模和影响力最大的旅游业综合性展会。ITB 被称作是整个旅游业的黄金市场，也是全球旅游行业首要的商务平台，已成为旅游业的"奥林匹克"。

ITB is the abbreviation of International Tourism Exchange. ITB Berlin is the largest and most influential tourism comprehensive exhibition in the world. ITB is known as the golden market for the entire tourism industry and the primary business platform for the global tourism industry. It has become the "Olympic" of the tourism industry.

1.2.8 IAEM

国际展览会管理协会（IAEM）成立于 1928 年，总部在美国。该协会与国际展览联盟（UFI）在国际展览界均享有盛誉，被认为是目前国际展览业最重要的行业组织。其成员来自 46 个国家或地区，数量超过 3,500 个。

The International Association for Exhibition Management (IAEM) was founded in 1928 and headquartered in the United States. IAEM and UFI enjoy high reputation in the international exhibition industry, and are considered as the most important industry organizations in the international exhibition industry. Members of IAEM come from 46 countries or regions and the number exceeds 3,500.

1.2.9 CMIC

中国会议产业大会（CMIC）旨在打造中国会议产业的年度盛会和行业平台。通过聚集行业力量及创新和创意的方式，进行观点交流和思想碰撞，推动中国会奖业的创新及发展。大会至今已经举办十三届，成为行业内标志性品牌活动。

China Meetings Industry Convention (CMIC) aims to create an annual event and industry platform for China's conference industry. By gathering industry forces and innovation and creativity, exchange views and magnetic collision of ideas, so as to promote the innovation and development of China's MICE industry. So far, it has been held for 13 times and has become a landmark brand activity in the industry.

1.2.10 PCO

PCO 是专业会议组织者的简称。专业会议组织者是会展业的核心，在国际上主要是指为筹办会议、展览及有关活动提供专业服务的公司，或从事相关工作的个人。

PCO is the abbreviation of Professional Conference Organizer. Professional conference organizers are the core of the convention and exhibition industry. Internationally, they mainly refer to companies that provide professional services for the preparation of conferences, exhibitions, and related activities, or individuals engaged in related work.

1.2.11 DMC

目的地管理公司（DMC）负责会展活动在主办地的现场协调会务和旅行安排等工作。

The Destination Management Company (DMC) is responsible for the on-site coordination and travel arrangement of the exhibition.

2 中国境内会奖目的地城市
MICE Destination Cities in China

2.1 中国北京概况
An Overview of Beijing, China

　　北京是中华人民共和国的首都、直辖市，是一个超大城市，是全国政治、文化中心，也是国际交往及科技创新中心。北京市总面积 16,410 平方千米，分成 16 个区 2 个县。截至 2020 年 11 月 1 日，北京市常住人口 2,189.3 万人。1949 年 10 月 1 日，北京成为中华人民共和国首都。2019 年 1 月 11 日，北京市级行政中心正式迁入北京城市副中心。北京被世界权威机构 GaWC 评为世界一线城市。

Beijing is the capital of the People's Republic of China, a municipality, super city, and the center of national politics and culture, as well as the center of international exchanges and technological innovation. The total area of Beijing is 16,410 square kilometers, divided into 16 districts and 2 counties. By Noverber 1, 2020, Beijing had 21.893 million permanent residents. It has been the capital of the People's Republic of China since October 1, 1949. On January 11, 2019, Beijing Municipal Administrative Center was officially moved to its Sub-center. Beijing is rated as the world's first tier city by a world's authoritative organization, GaWC.

2.1.1　气候 /Climate
　　北京为典型的大陆性季风气候，四季分明，春秋短促，温度宜人。夏季高温多雨，南北温差小；冬季寒冷干燥，南北温差偏大。

Beijing has a typical continental monsoon climate with four distinct seasons: short spring and autumn seasons with pleasant temperatures; hot and rainy summer with small temperature difference between north and south; cold and dry winter with larger temperature difference between north and south.

2.1.2 交通 /Transportation

北京有两个民用机场，即北京首都国际机场和北京大兴国际机场。北京首都国际机场（顺义）4F级民用机场，为世界超大型机场，距离市中心25千米，是中国三大门户复合枢纽之一，分为3个航站楼：T1、T2、T3。北京大兴国际机场，4F级民用机场，大型国际航空枢纽，位于中国北京市大兴区与河北省廊坊市交界，距离首都机场67千米，2019年9月机场正式投入运营，共开通国内外航线119条。北京共有5座火车站，即北京站、北京南站、北京西站、北京东站和北京北站，北京的交通压力很大。

There are two civil airports in Beijing, namely Beijing Capital International Airport and Beijing Daxing International Airport. Beijing Capital International Airport (Shunyi) is a 4F-class civil airport and one of the world's largest airports. It's 25 kilometers away from city center and one of the three major compound hubs in China, divided into three terminals: T1, T2, T3. Beijing Daxing International Airport, also a 4F-class civil airport, located on the border of Daxing District, Beijing and Langfang, Hebei Province, 67 kilometers away from the Capital Airport, is an international aviation hub. In September 2019, the airport officially started operation, opening 119 domestic and foreign routes. There are 5 railway stations in Beijing: Beijing Railway Station, Beijing South Railway Station, Beijing West Railway Station, Beijing East Railway Station, and Beijing North Railway Station. Beijing suffers high pressure in transportation.

2.1.3 展馆与酒店 /Exhibition Venues and Hotels

北京各类展馆丰富，容纳能力已达到亚太地区领先水平，为北京发展会奖旅游提供了必要的基础设施；北京具有完善的高端旅游住宿、餐饮和交通，为北京接待高端商务会奖游客提供了便利条件。国家会议中心在2008年奥运会期间是文字记者和摄影记者的工作区，2014 年是 APEC 主会场，已成为世界级的会展品牌。中国国际展览中心为 UFI 在中国的首个成员和 IAEM 会员。北京国际会议中心是 ICCA 在中国的第一家会员。截至 2019 年底，北京共有五星级酒店 131 家。

Beijing is rich in various types of exhibition venues, whose capacity have reached the leading level in the Asia-Pacific region, providing the necessary infrastructure for Beijing to develop MICE tourism. Having excellent high-end tourism accommodation, catering and transportation, Beijing can welcome senior business MICE tourists. During the 2008 Olympic Games, the National Convention Center was a working area for journalists and photojournalists. In 2014, it was the main venue of APEC, and it has become a world-class exhibition brand. China International Exhibition Center is the first member of UFI in China and a member of IAEM. The Beijing International Convention Center is the first member of ICCA in China. By the end of 2019, there were 131 five-star hotels in Beijing.

2.1.4 会奖目的地优势 /Advantages of MICE Destination

拥有会奖旅游"先天优势"的北京，会奖之都模式已初现规模。北京成为越来越多国际会议和展览青睐的目的地城市，并朝着"会奖之都"的目标迈进。2016 年北京举办 ICCA 认证的国际会议 113 个，2017 年 81 个，2018 年 93 个，2019 年 91 个。随着大兴国际机场和城市副中心的投入使用，周边会奖旅游设施及商务配套项目建设在稳步推进中，未来 3~5 年北京的会奖旅游承载力将大幅提升。

Beijing, which has the "excellent gene" of MICE tourism, has already begun to take shape of MICE capital mode. Becoming a destination city favored by more and more international conferences and exhibitions, Beijing is moving towards the goal of "MICE capital". Beijing held 113 ICCA-certified international conferences in 2016, 81 in 2017, 93 in 2018, and 91 in 2019. With the opening of Daxing International Airport and the city sub-center, the surrounding MICE facilities and supporting business projects being construction, the capacity of Beijing's MICE tourism in the next 3 to 5 years will be greatly improved.

◎特色旅游资源/Unique Tourism Resources

北京历史悠久，文化灿烂，是首批国家历史文化名城之一、中国四大古都之一，以及世界上拥有世界文化遗产数最多的城市。3,000多年的建城史孕育了众多名胜古迹。周口店北京猿人遗址、八达岭长城、故宫、颐和园、天坛、明十三陵、中国大运河这7个地方被列为世界文化遗产。这座高度现代化的城市充满了古典文化的气息，令人心驰神往：走进故宫，仿佛穿越到了古代；爬上长城，可以触摸历经几千年风雨冲刷的城墙；城内的每一条胡同、每一座四合院都承载了历史和故事。

Beijing has a long history and splendid culture. It is one of the first national historical and cultural cities, one of the four ancient capitals in China, and the city with the largest number of world cultural heritage in the world. The history of the city's construction of more than 3,000 years has bred many scenic spots and historic sites. Seven places including Zhoukoudian Peking Man Site, Badaling Great Wall, Forbidden City, Summer Palace, Temple of Heaven, Ming Tombs, and China Grand Canal are listed as World Cultural Heritage. This modern city is filled with the fascinating atmosphere of classical culture: Walking into the Forbidden City, it seems that you have crossed into the ancient times; climbing the Great Wall, you can touch the wall that has been washed by wind and rain for thousands of years; every courtyard and Hutong in the city carries history and stories.

◎世界一线城市 /The World's First-tier City

北京被世界权威机构 GaWC 评为世界一线城市。北京的综合经济实力、对人才的吸引力、国际竞争力、科技创新和信息交流能力等都起到引领和辐射的作用。北京大学和清华大学是中国最顶尖的两所大学，也是北京的两张金名片。

Beijing is rated as the world's first-tier city by GaWC which is a world's authoritative organization. Beijing's comprehensive economic capabilities, attractiveness to talents, international competitiveness, technological innovation and information exchange capabilities, etc. play a leading and radiating role to other cities. Peking University and Tsinghua University are the two top universities in China, and they are also the two golden cards of Beijing.

◎独角兽之都 /Unicorn Capital

根据 2019 年《财富》杂志公布的世界 500 强企业名单，56 家世界 500 强企业总部位于北京，位列全球第一。近 5 年来，市值超过 10 亿美元的独角兽企业在北京如雨后春笋般诞生、聚集、成长。创新成为北京城市活力的源泉，也使得北京取代旧金山成为独角兽之都。

According to the list of Fortune Global 500 published by *Fortune* in 2019, 56 headquarters of Fortune Global 500 corporations are in Beijing, ranking first in the world. In the past five years, unicorn companies with a market value of more than 1 billion US dollars have sprung up, gathered, and grown in Beijing. Innovation has become the source of vitality in Beijing, and enables Beijing to replace San Francisco as the capital of unicorn companies.

2.2 中国上海概况
An Overview of Shanghai, China

上海是中国 4 个直辖市之一，是中国经济、金融、贸易、航运、科技创新中心。上海位于中国华东地区，地处长江入海口，上海市总面积 6,340.5 平方千米。截至 2020 年底，全市常住人口总数约为 2487.09 万人。上海既是中国第一大城市，也是一座享誉世界的国际大都市。它拥有中国最大的外贸港口和最大的工业基地；拥有深厚的近代城市文化底蕴和众多的历史古迹。它是一座充满着机遇与挑战的魔力之都。

Shanghai is one of the four municipalities directly under the Central Government, and it is also a center of economy, finance, trade, shipping, and technological innovation in China. Shanghai is located in the East China region, at the mouth of the Yangtze River, with a total area of 6,340.5 square kilometers. By the end of 2020, the total resident population of the city was 24.8709 million. Shanghai is both China's largest city and a world-renowned international metropolis. It has China's largest foreign trade port and China's largest industrial base; it has profound modern urban cultural heritage and numerous historical monuments. It is a magical capital full of opportunities and challenges.

2.2.1 气候 /Climate

上海属亚热带季风性气候，四季分明，日照充分，雨量充沛。上海气候温和湿润，春秋较短，冬夏较长。

Shanghai has a subtropical monsoon climate with four distinct seasons, sufficient sunshine, and abundant rainfall. It has a mild and humid climate, with shorter spring and autumn, and longer winter and summer.

2.2.2 交通 /Transportation

浦东是上海重要的交通枢纽。先进的国际物流港口、航空运输、铁路轨道运输、城际高速路共同建构了水、陆、空三位一体的交通体系。浦江大桥、海底隧道、磁悬浮列车、地铁线路织成密集的交通网络。上海拥有两座民用机场：4E 级的上海虹桥国际机场和 4F 级的上海浦东国际机场。上海共有三大火车站：上海火车站、上海虹桥火车站、上海南火车站，其中上海虹桥火车站是上海最大、最现代化的铁路客运站。

Pudong is an important transportation hub in Shanghai. An advanced international logistics port, air transportation, railway transportation, and intercity highways jointly build a trinity transportation system of water, land, and air. Pujiang Bridge, undersea tunnel, maglev train, and subway lines form dense transportation network. Shanghai has two civil airports: 4E-class Shanghai Hongqiao International Airport and 4F-class Shanghai Pudong International Airport. There are three major railway stations in Shanghai: Shanghai Railway Station, Shanghai Hongqiao Railway Station, and Shanghai South Railway Station. Shanghai Hongqiao Railway Station is the largest and most modern railway passenger station in Shanghai.

2.2.3 展馆与酒店 /Exhibition Venues and Hotels

上海建有多个会展场馆，其中体量最大、知名度最高、影响力最大的四大展馆为国家会展中心（上海）、上海新国际博览中心、上海世博展览馆、上海国际展览中心。国家会展中心（上海）是目前世界上面积第二大的建筑单体和会展综合体，仅次于德国的汉诺威会展中心，总建筑面积 147 万平方米。上海各类专业展馆可供展览的面积已超过 100 万平方米。2018 年上海已拥有 UFI 认证的展览项目 23 个，是国内获得认证最多的城市。上海展览数量和展览面积等多项指标均居国内首位，跻身世界前列。上海豪华型酒店及经济型酒店繁多，可以满足不同层次的住宿需求。

There are many exhibition venues in Shanghai, among which the four largest ones with the largest volume, the highest visibility, and the most influence are the National Exhibition and Convention Center (Shanghai), Shanghai New International Expo Center, Shanghai World Expo Exhibition & Convention Center, and INTEX Shanghai Exhibition Center. National Exhibition and Convention Center (Shanghai) is currently the second largest building monomer and exhibition complex in the world, second only to the Hanover Exhibition and Convention Center in Germany, with a total construction area of 1.47 million square meters. All kinds of professional exhibition venues in Shanghai have a total exhibition area of more than 1 million square meters. In 2018, Shanghai already had 23 exhibition projects certified by the UFI, making it the most certified city in China. Many indicators such as the number of exhibitions and exhibition area in Shanghai rank first in China and is among the top in the world. There are many luxury hotels and budget hotels in Shanghai, which can meet the needs of different levels of accommodation.

2.2.4 会奖目的地优势 /Advantages of MICE Destination

上海拥有多个会展场馆、一应俱全的高中低档酒店、便利的交通条件、丰富的办会经验和都市旅游资源等，使得上海在会奖目的地竞争中极具优势。2010 年的上海世博会成为有史以来最引人瞩目、最非凡的世博会之一，园区面积之大，参展、观展者数量之多，都创下百年世博的全新纪录。2016 年上海迪士尼度假区的成功开园更为上海市的会奖旅游产业提供了一个实现跨越式发展的巨大历史机遇。2017—2019 年上海共承办 ICCA 认证的国际会议 230 个。上海必将成为最有潜质的会奖目的地城市之一。

Shanghai has many exhibition venues, a variety choices of hotels, convenient transportation conditions, rich experience in organizing conventions, and urban tourism resources, etc., which makes Shanghai very advantageous in the competition of MICE destinations. The 2010 Shanghai World Expos was one of the most eye-catching and extraordinary World Expos ever. The area of the park, the number of exhibitors and visitors all set a record for the 100-year World Expo. The opening of the Shanghai Disney Resort in 2016 provided a historical opportunity for the Shanghai MICE Industry to achieve leap-frog development. From 2017 to 2019, Shanghai hosted 230 ICCA-certified international conferences. Shanghai is bound to become one of the most promising MICE destination cities.

◎特色旅游资源/Unique Tourism Resources：上海迪士尼度假区 /Shanghai Disney Resort

上海迪士尼度假区拥有全球迪士尼乐园最先进的技术、最大和最高的城堡，以及首个以海盗为主题的园区。这座无与伦比的主题乐园以全球魔法迎接广大游客，为大家带去迪士尼的神奇体验和天马行空的想象力。探险岛、奇想花园、米奇大街、明日世界、宝藏湾、梦幻世界等六大园区带你玩转会奖旅游活动。迪士尼园区各大剧院把世界级水准的娱乐演出带到了中国：百老汇音乐剧《美女与野兽》百看不厌，《风暴来临》惊心动魄，米奇童话专列巡游则令人童心萌发。上海迪士尼度假区融合了永无止境的创新和闻名于世的创意，为客人提供了一个"原汁原味迪士尼、别具一格中国风"的神奇且独特的会奖目的地。

Shanghai Disney Resort has the most advanced technology, the largest and tallest castle, and the first pirate-themed park. This unparalleled theme park welcomes visitors with magic, bringing Disney's magical experience and boundless imagination. Six major parks including Adventure Island, Wonderland Garden, Mickey Avenue, Tomorrow Land, Treasure Bay, and Dream World make visitors fully enjoy all kinds of MICE activities. The major theaters in the park bring world-class entertainment performances to China: Broadway musical *Beauty and Beast* is never tiresome, *The Storm Is Coming* is thrilling,

and Mickey's Fairy Tale parade will take you back to sweet childhood. Shanghai Disney Resort combines the endless innovation and the world-renowned creativity, providing the guests with a magical and special MICE destination of "Original Disney, Unique Chinese Style".

◎精彩夜上海 /Wonderful Night in Shanghai

上海外滩曾经是法租界，在这里可以欣赏精美的外国建筑群，也可以感受黄浦江边柔美的风景。外滩是上海骄傲和屈辱历史的代表，见证了旧上海全盛时期的辉煌和被外国人占领的悲伤。上海最具魔力的地方之一是越夜越精彩，越夜越文艺：黄浦江两岸的灯光秀形成了一幅美轮美奂的绝美画卷，陆家嘴高楼林立、鳞次栉比、流光溢彩；你可以去美术馆感受超级"魔法"世界，也可以去麦金侬酒店看一场大型莎翁沉浸式戏剧，或者去"时相遇·1913百年茶馆"品茗喝茶，仿佛穿越时空回到民国时期。

The Bund used to be the French Concession, where you can admire exquisite foreign buildings and feel the beautiful scenery along the Huangpu River. The Bund is a representative of Shanghai's history of pride and humiliation, witnessing the glory of old Shanghai during its heyday and the sadness of being occupied by foreigners. One of the most magical aspects of Shanghai is that it gets more wonderful and literary as the night gets later: the lighting show on both sides of the Huangpu River forms a magnificent picture, skyscrapers in Lujiazui create a unique view with amazing lighting. You can go to Art Gallery to feel the "magic" world, or go to the McKinnon Hotel to enjoy a Shakespeare's immersive drama, or go to "Shixiangyu·1913 Centennial Tea House" to have a time travel while enjoying tea.

◎国际金融中心/International Financial Center

2019年上海保持了全球第五大国际金融中心城市的地位，仅次于纽约、伦敦、香港、新加坡。这是上海继2018年后第二次在全球金融中心指数（GFCI）排名中位居全球金融中心的前五位，2017年上海首次进入全球前十。上海目前建立了较为完备的金融市场体系，集聚了一大批中外资金融机构，成为中国大陆金融对外开放的最前沿、金融改革创新的先行区。自2013年中国（上海）自由贸易试验区成立，其吸引外资的势头强劲。

In 2019, Shanghai remained the fifth largest international financial center in the world, second only to New York, London, Hong Kong, and Singapore. This is the second time that Shanghai has ranked among the top five global financial centers in the Global Financial Centers Index (GFCI) ranking after 2018. In 2017, Shanghai ranked in the top 10 for the first time. At present, Shanghai has established a relatively complete financial market system, and has gathered many Chinese and foreign financial institutions, becoming the forefront of Mailand China's finance opening to the outside world, and the pioneer area of financial reform and innovation. Since the establishment of China (Shanghai) Pilot Free Trade Zone in 2013, the momentum of attracting foreign investment has been strong.

2.3 中国杭州概况
An Overview of Hangzhou, China

杭州是浙江省的省会和副省级城市，是环杭州湾大湾区核心城市、国际重要的电子商务中心。截至 2020 年 11 月 1 日，全市下辖 10 个区、2 个县、1 个县级市，总面积 16,850 平方千米，建成区面积 559.2 平方千米，常住人口 1,193.6 万人。

Hangzhou is the capital and sub-provincial city of Zhejiang Province. It is the core city of the Greater Bay Area around Hangzhou Bay and an important international e-commerce center. By November 1, 2020, the city has 10 districts, 2 counties, and 1 county-level city under its jurisdiction, with a total area of 16,850 square kilometers, a built-up area of 559.2 square kilometers, and a permanent population of 11.936 million.

2.3.1 气候 /Climate

杭州地处长江三角洲南沿和钱塘江流域，地形复杂多样。杭州市西部以丘陵为主，东部地势低平，河网及湖泊密布。杭州属于亚热带季风气候，四季分明，雨量充沛。

Hangzhou is located in the south of the Yangtze River Delta and the Qiantang River Basin, with complex and diverse terrain. The west of Hangzhou is dominated by hills, and the east is low and flat, with dense river networks and lakes. Hangzhou has a subtropical monsoon climate with four distinct seasons and abundant rainfall.

2.3.2　交通/Transportation

杭州萧山国际机场，4F 级机场，距市中心 27 千米，是中国十二大干线机场之一。杭州目前有 3 座火车站：杭州站、杭州东站、杭州南站，杭州西站在建。杭州东站是杭州市接驳功能最为齐全的交通枢纽，是中国大型铁路枢纽站之一。2022 年亚运会之前开通 14 条地铁。

Hangzhou Xiaoshan International Airport, a 4F-class airport, 27 kilometers away from the city center, is one of the 12 major trunk airports in China. There are 3 railway stations in Hangzhou now: Hangzhou Station, Hangzhou East Station, and Hangzhou South Station, while Hangzhou West Station is under construction. Hangzhou East Railway Station is the transportation hub with the most complete connection function in Hangzhou and one of the largest railway hub stations in China. 14 subways will be completed before the 2022 Asian Games.

2.3.3　展馆与酒店/Exhibition Venues and Hotels

杭州市目前最大的会展展览场馆是杭州国际博览中心，它曾是 G20 峰会的主场地。杭州白马湖国际会展中心是杭州乃至全国规模最大、产业基础最优越的文化创意产业集聚区。杭州未来 3 年规划建设展览面积 30 万平方米的专业展馆，集会展园区、商务旅游、休闲购物于一体。杭州已初步形成环西湖、武林、黄龙、钱江新城、西溪天堂、千岛湖等 10 个板块的会议酒店集群。无论是大型国际会议、精品定制小会，还是连会带展，杭州都可以满足客户的需求。

The largest exhibition venue in Hangzhou is the Hangzhou International Expo Center, which was the main venue of the G20 Summit. The Hangzhou Baimahu International Exhibition Center is the largest cultural and creative industry gathering area with the most superior industrial foundation in Hangzhou and even in the whole country. Hangzhou plans to build a professional exhibition venue with an exhibition area of 300,000 square meters in the next three years, integrating exhibition parks, business tourism, and leisure shopping. Hangzhou has initially formed a conference hotel cluster of 10 segments including West

Lake, Wulin, Huanglong, Qianjiang New Town, Xixi Paradise, and Qiandao Lake, etc. Hangzhou can fully satisfy customers' needs, whether it is a large international conference, a boutique custom-made small meeting, or even a conference with exhibition.

2.3.4　会奖目的地优势 /Advantages of MICE Destination

2016 年 G20 峰会和 2018 年世界短池游泳锦标赛给杭州带来极大的国际效应，让杭州成为会奖业冉冉升起的一颗明珠。杭州凭借 2018 年 28 个、2019 年 38 个 ICCA 认证的国际会议，位列城市排名中国大陆城市第三。2019 年杭州荣获 "MICE STARS 会奖之星——2019 中国最具创新力国际会奖目的地" 奖项。10 年来，杭州一共举办了 214 个国际会议，参会者总数达近 6 万人次，杭州会奖旅游业发展迅速。

The 2016 G20 Summit and the 2018 FINA Short Course World Championships have brought great international influence to Hangzhou, making it a rising pearl of the MICE industry. With 28 ICCA-certified international conferences, Hangzhou ranked third in Mainland China in 2018. In 2019, Hangzhou hosted 38 ICCA-certified international conferences and won the "MICE STARS—2019 China's Most Innovative International MICE Destination" award. Over the past ten years, Hangzhou has held a total of 214 international conferences with nearly 60,000 participants. Hangzhou's MICE industry has developed rapidly.

◎特色旅游资源/Unique Tourism Resources

杭州人文古迹众多。西湖及其周边有大量的自然与人文景观遗迹，具代表性的有西湖文化、良渚文化、丝绸文化、茶文化，以及流传下来的许多故事传说。杭州几千年来因风景秀丽，素有 "人间天堂" 的美誉。西湖随着四季的变换而有不同的风貌，如一幅幅天然的画作，更像一首首动人的诗篇；京杭大运河是流动的中华文明，是休闲的天堂画卷，让外国人领略 "中国"，中国人感受 "杭州"，年轻人体验 "时尚"；良渚古城遗址带你穿越时空，感受中华文明五千年的璀璨之光。杭州西湖、杭州京杭大运河、杭州良渚古城遗址等三大世界文化遗产成为杭州的 3 张金名片。

There are many cultural and historic sites in Hangzhou. A lot of natural and cultural landscapes are around West Lake. Representatives include West Lake culture, Liangzhu culture, silk culture, tea culture, and many stories and legends that have been handed down. Hangzhou is known as the "Paradise on Earth" for its beautiful scenery. The West Lake has different styles as the season changes, with the scenery like natural paintings and touching poems; the Beijing-Hangzhou Grand Canal is a flowing Chinese civilization, a leisure paradise scroll that allows foreigners to appreciate "China", Chinese people feel "Hangzhou", and young people experience "fashion"; the Archaeological take you through time and space, and make you feel the glory of the Chinese civilization for five thousand years. Three major world cultural heritage such as West Lake, Beijing-Hangzhou Grand Canal, and Ruins of Liangzhu City have become three golden business cards of Hangzhou.

◎国际组织永久落户杭州/International Organizations Permanently Settled in Hangzhou

世界旅游联盟（WTA）总部、全球可持续发展标准化城市联盟、国际标准化会议基地、联合国教科文组织的项目事务处、国际丝绸联盟总部（ISU）、"一带一路"国际联盟总部等落户杭州。杭州都市圈范围内的乌镇也成为世界互联网大会永久会址。杭州凭借优美的环境和独特的文化，将吸引越来越多的国际组织和国际公共机构入驻，借此主办国际性会议的数量将会大大增加，城市的认可度和美誉度也会得到大力提升。国际组织和机构的落户对助推杭州成为国际会奖旅游之都意义非凡。

The headquarter of the World Tourism Alliance (WTA), the Global Sustainable Standardization City Alliance, the International Standardization Conference Base, the UNESCO Project Office, the International Silk Union Headquarter (ISU), and the headquarter of "Belt and Road" International Alliance have settled in Hangzhou. And within Hangzhou metropolitan area, Wuzhen has also become the permanent address for the World Internet Conference. With its beautiful environment and unique culture,

Hangzhou will attract more and more international organizations and public institutions. The number of international conferences will greatly increase and the city's recognition and reputation will also be greatly improved. The settlement of international organizations and institutions is of great significance to promote Hangzhou as an international MICE tourism capital.

◎独角兽企业众多/Numerous Unicorn Companies

作为会奖旅游业发展的重要支撑，杭州大批独角兽企业崛起，估值 10 亿美元以上的企业有 30 家，在独角兽估值总额上超过上海位居全国第二。杭州独角兽企业遍地开花，势必吸引与独角兽企业相关的全球著名投资机构、券商、律所、孵化器、银行等创业、投资服务各环节的品牌企业进驻杭州。独角兽企业在产业链中的引领和平台作用势必吸引有影响力的国际会议，如 2016 第八届世界两栖动物学大会、2018 第四届国际文化遗产研究大会等在杭州召开，从而带动区域经济的发展。

As an important support for the development of MICE industry, many unicorn companies in Hangzhou have risen. There are 30 companies valued at more than 1 billion US dollars in Hangzhou, ranking second in the whole country in terms of total valuation over Shanghai. Hangzhou unicorn companies are blooming everywhere, and it is bound to attract world-renowned investment institutions, brokers, law firms, incubators, banks and other brand-name enterprises in the links of entrepreneurship and investment services. The leading and platform role of the unicorn companies is bound to attract influential international conferences to be held in Hangzhou, such as the 8th World Amphibian Conference in 2016 and the 4th International Cultural Heritage Research Conference in 2018, thereby driving the development of regional economy.

2.4 中国成都概况
An Overview of Chengdu, China

中国成都

成都是四川省省会、副省级城市、特大城市、西部地区重要的中心城市，幅员面积 14,335 平方千米，常住人口 1,658.10 万人（2020 年）。成都位于中国西南地区，四川盆地西部。地势由西北向东南倾斜。成都平原腹地地势平坦、河网纵横，自古享有"天府之国"的美誉。

Chengdu is the capital of Sichuan Province, a sub-provincial city, a megacity, and an important central city in the western region, with an area of 14,335 square kilometers and a permanent population of 16.5810 million (2020). Chengdu is in the southwest of China and the west of the Sichuan Basin. The terrain slopes from northwest to southeast. The hinterland of the Chengdu Plain has a flat terrain and a complex river network. It has been known as the "Land of Heaven" since ancient times.

2.4.1 气候/Climate

成都属亚热带季风性气候，具有春早、夏热、秋凉、冬暖的气候特点。多云雾，空气潮湿，日照时间短。

Chengdu has a subtropical monsoon climate with the characteristics of early spring, hot summer, cool autumn, and warm winter. It has cloudy fog, humid air, and short time of sunshine.

2.4.2 交通 /Transportation

构建外部联通、内部贯通的交通网络，加快建设中国西部综合交通枢纽，是成都推动会奖产业的一大举措。成都双流国际机场，4F 机场，是中西部第一、全国第四大机场，距离成都市区 16 千米。成都有 3 座火车站，其中成都东站是中西部最大的铁路客运站之一，是集铁路、轨道、客运、公交等多种交通方式于一体的综合交通枢纽。便捷的交通有效地节省了会奖活动成本。

Constructing an externally and internally connected transportation network, and accelerating the construction of a comprehensive transportation hub in western China, is a major move for Chengdu to promote the MICE industry. Chengdu Shuangliu International Airport, 4F-class airport, has become the first airport in the midwest and the fourth largest in the country, 16 kilometers away from city center. Chengdu has 3 railway stations, of which Chengdu East Station is one of the largest railway passenger stations in the midwest. It is a comprehensive transportation hub integrating railway, subway, long-distance bus, city public bus, and other transportation modes. Convenient transportation effectively saves MICE activity costs.

2.4.3 展馆与酒店 /Exhibition Venues and Hotels

成都主要的展馆有成都世纪城新国际展览中心、中国西部国际博览城国际展览展示中心、成都国际会议展览中心和四川省展览馆。成都世纪城新国际会展中心是目前中国西部建筑规模最大、功能配套最完备、设施最先进的多功能会议会展中心。成都共有 18 家五星级酒店，西南首家 W 酒店于 2020 年 10 月开业。

The main exhibition venues in Chengdu are Chengdu Century City New International Convertion and Exhibition Center, International Exhibition Center of Western China International Expo City, Chengdu International Conference and Exhibition Center, and Sichuan Exhibition Hall. Chengdu Century City New International Convention and Exhibition Center has currently the largest construction scale and the most complete functional facilities, and is the most advanced multi-functional conference and exhibition

center in Western China. There are 18 5-star hotels in Chengdu, and the first W hotel in Southwest China opened in October 2020.

2.4.4　会奖目的地优势 /Advantages of MICE Destination

成都曾获得"2017 年度'一带一路'最具活力城市""2018 中国最具投资吸引力城市""2019 年联合国教科文组织学习型城市奖"等奖项。2016 年到 2019 年共举办 ICCA 认证的国际会议 98 个。

Chengdu has won "The Most Dynamic City along the Belt and Road in 2017" "The Most Attractive City in China in 2018", and "UNESCO Learning City Award in 2019". From 2016 to 2019, 98 international conferences on ICCA certification were held in Chengdu.

◎特色旅游资源/Unique Tourism Resources

成都有众多的自然和人文景观，包括世界自然文化遗产——青城山—都江堰、峨眉山—乐山大佛、九寨沟、黄龙、大熊猫栖息地等。同时，在市区打造了民俗文化旅游餐饮街区——宽窄巷子和锦里，以及东区音乐公园。美食、美景为会议后旅游提供了多元化的选择。成都还打造了大英死海，以漂浮和黑泥浴而闻名。这是一种运用现代科技手段与时尚旅游要素创造出的全新的旅游概念和旅游方式，是传统与时尚、资源与科技完美结合的新一代旅游产品。

Chengdu has many natural and cultural landscapes, including the world's natural and cultural heritage—Qingcheng Mountain-Dujiangyan, Emei Mountain-Leshan Giant Buddha, Jiuzhaigou, Huanglong, Giant Panda Habitat, etc. At the same time, folk culture, tourism and catering districts are built in the urban area—Kuanzhai Alley and Jinli, as well as the East District Music Park. Food and scenery provide diversified options for post-conference tourism. Chengdu has also created the "Dead Sea", known for its floating and black mud baths. It has created a brand-new travel concept and method using modern technology and fashionable tourism elements. It is a new generation of travel product, combining tradition and fashion, resources and technology.

◎中国最具幸福感城市榜首/The Happiest City in China

成都已经连续十多年蝉联"中国最具幸福感城市"榜首。成都人讲究自然、休闲，以及人与自然和谐相处。身处平原中心的成都人，没有穷山恶水的困扰，也没有大江大河的冲击，富庶的生活让每个人由内而外散发出一种招人嫉妒的慵懒。任何一次慵懒的机会，成都人都不会放过：坐在阳台上，望得见雪山；下楼走走，那是全球最长的绿道；转角，不是茶馆就是各色美食。成都拥有中国数量第一的茶馆，成都的茶馆数量有近万家之多。成都还拥有中国第二多的书店和酒吧。

Chengdu has been ranked first in the list of "China's Happiest Cities" for more than ten consecutive years. People in Chengdu focus on nature, leisure, and harmony between man and nature. The people of Chengdu, who live in the center of the plain, are free from the turbulence of high mountains and river floods. The prosperous life allows everyone to have a life style of indolence. Chengdu people will never miss an opportunity to be "lazy": sitting on the balcony, you can see the snowy mountains; walking downstairs, you will be on the longest green road in the world; going around the corner, it is possible to encounter a tea house or a variety of delicious food. Chengdu has the largest number of tea houses in China, nearly 10,000 ones. The city also has the second largest number of bookstores and bars in China.

◎主打"三城三都"/Three Cities and Three Capitals

成都主打"三城三都"——世界文创名城、赛事名城、旅游名城和国际美食之都、音乐之都、会展之都，并取得了显著成效。成都每年举办众多的大型展会，如糖酒会、国际车展、西博会等。不少国际知名展会亦选择落户成都，如集成专业视听和体验的商贸展览会 InfoComm、财富全球论坛、福布斯中国创新峰会、世界警察大会、国际马拉松等，这些展会创造出更多不同类型的商机，也让成都在全球会奖市场中的口碑大放光彩；众多大型外资企业如 IBM、英特尔、微软、澳新银行等进驻成都，也带动了企业商旅市场的蓬勃发展。

Chengdu's focus on "Three Cities and Three Capitals"—the world's cultural and creative city, event city, tourism city, and international gourmet capital, music capital, convention and exhibition capital, have achieved remarkable results. Every year, Chengdu holds many large-scale exhibitions, such as the Sugar and Liquor Fair, the International Auto Show, and the West Expo. Many internationally renowned exhibitions also choose to settle in Chengdu, such as InfoComm, Fortune Global Forum, Forbes China Innovation Summit, The World Police Congress, and the International Marathon. It has created different types of business opportunities, and improved Chengdu's reputation in the global MICE market. The opening of many large foreign enterprises such as IBM, Intel, Microsoft, ANZ also promotes the development of business travel market.

2.5 中国西安概况
An Overview of Xi'an, China

西安是陕西省省会和丝绸之路的起点。西安是世界四大古都之一，也是中国历史上建都朝代最多、时间最长、影响力最大的都城之一。其总面积 10,752 平方千米，2020 年底常住人口 1,295.29 万人。西安地处关中平原中部。群峰竞秀的秦岭山地与平畴沃野的渭河平原，构成西安市的地貌主体。

Xi'an is the capital of Shaanxi Province and the starting point of the Silk Road. It is one of the four ancient capitals in the world, and one of the capitals with the most dynasties, the longest time, and the most influence in the history of China. With a total area of 10,752 square kilometers, the permanent population is 12.9529 million by the end of 2020. Xi'an is in the middle of the Guanzhong Plain. The Qinling Mountains and the Weihe Plain together form the distinct landforms in Xi'an.

2.5.1 气候/Climate

西安属暖温带半湿润大陆性季风气候，冷暖干湿四季分明。冬季寒冷、少雨雪；春季气候多变；夏季炎热多雨；秋季凉爽，气温速降。

Xi'an has a warm temperate and semi-humid continental monsoon climate, with four distinct seasons characterized by cold, warm, dry, and wet weather. It is cold in winter with less rain and snow; it is changeable in spring; it is hot and rainy in summer; it is cool in autumn and the temperature drops rapidly.

2.5.2 交通 /Transportation

西安咸阳国际机场，4F 级机场，距西安市区 25 千米，是中国八大区域枢纽机场之一。西安已开通 339 条航线，其中国际航线 57 条，可直达 47 个国家和地区。随着高铁的快速兴建，预计 2025 年陕西省将纳入全国 3 小时经济圈。西安有 3 座火车站：西安站、西安南站和西安北站，西安站是主火车站。地铁线路共有 5 条，分别为：1 号线、2 号线、3 号线、4 号线、机场城际线。

Xi'an Xianyang International Airport, a 4F-class airport, 25 kilometers away from city center, is one of China's eight regional hub airports. Xi'an has opened 339 routes, including 57 international routes, which can reach 47 countries and regions. With the rapid construction of high-speed rail, Shaanxi Province is expected to be included in the national 3-hour economic circle in 2025. There are 3 railway stations in Xi'an: Xi'an Station, Xi'an South Station, and Xi'an North Station. Xi'an Station is the main railway station. There are 5 metro lines: Line 1, Line 2, Line 3, Line 4, and Airport Intercity Line.

2.5.3 展馆与酒店 /Exhibition Venues and Hotels

西安丝路国际会展中心分为会议中心、展览中心两个项目，是集会、展、节、赛、演于一体的会展中心，总建筑面积约 100 万平方米。建成后，它将填补西安及西北地区大型专业会议中心场馆的市场空白，可满足国际高峰论坛、双边及多边会议等大型会议和宴会的功能要求，也将成为丝绸之路高峰论坛永久会址及西北地区功能最齐备、面积最大的综合性会议中心。西安各类酒店相对国内一线城市价格显得亲民，但如何兼顾不同使用人群的需求是酒店业设计师进行人性化设计时应该考虑的因素。世界级的西安曲江国际会议中心、西安丝路国际会展中心及众多高星级酒店，可以为举办国际会议、会展提供高品质的保障。

Xi'an Silk Road International Convention and Exhibition Center is divided into two projects: a conference center and an exhibition center. It integrates conferences, exhibitions, festivals, competitions, and performances. The total construction area is about 1 million square meters. After completion, it will fill the market gap of large professional conference center venues in Xi'an and the northwest region, and meet the functional requirements of large conferences and banquets such as international summit forums, bilateral and multilateral conferences. It will also become the permanent meeting place of the Silk Road Summit Forum and the most versatile and largest comprehensive conference center in the northwest region. Compared with domestic first-tier cities, the prices of various hotels in Xi'an are cheaper. But how to meet the needs of different groups is a factor that hotel designers should consider. The world-class Xi'an Qujiang International Conference Center, Xi'an Silk Road International Convention and Exhibition Center, and many high-star hotels can provide high-quality guarantee for hosting international conferences and exhibitions.

2.5.4 会奖目的地优势 /Advantages of MICE Destination

据 ICCA 发布的统计报告，2016 年至 2019 年西安共承接 ICCA 认证的国际会议 99 个。一场知名的国际会议可以提高城市的知名度和美誉度，促进贸易与交流，带动当地第三产业的发展。近年来西安一直以建设"一带一路"国际会展名城为目标，不断完善机制、优化布局、提升会奖目的地城市的影响力。

According to the statistics released by ICCA, Xi'an has undertaken 99 international conferences certified by ICCA from 2016 to 2019. A well-known international conference can improve the reputation of the city, promote trade and exchanges, and drive the development of the local service industry. Xi'an has been building "The Belt and Road" international exhibition city as the goal in recent years, and constantly improving its mechanism, optimizing its layout, and enhancing the influence of MICE destination city.

◎特色旅游资源：13 朝古都、6 项世界文化遗产 /Unique Tourism Resources: The Ancient Capital of the 13 Dynasties and 6 World Cultural Heritage

西安是中华文明和中华民族的重要发祥地之一，历史上先后有 13 个王朝在此建都。千百年来，留下了许多古老珍贵的文化瑰宝。西安有 6 处遗产被列入《世界遗产名录》，分别是：秦始皇陵及兵马俑、大雁塔、小雁塔、唐长安城大明宫遗址、汉长安城未央宫遗址、兴教寺塔。西安是一部读不完的历史书，也是一堂讲不完的文化课。作为世界历史文化名城，西安的历史文化、丝路文化、盛世文化、红色文化、时尚文化等都彰显了中华民族最持久的文化自信，也为西安的会奖旅游业注入了灵魂。西安文化旅游资源丰富，优势突出，在"一带一路"倡议建设中，发展潜力巨大，是一片方兴未艾的投资热土。

Xi'an is one of the important birthplaces of the Chinese civilization and the Chinese nation. In history, capitals of 13 dynasties have been built here. For thousands of years, many ancient and precious cultural treasures have been kept here. Six properties in Xi'an have been included in the "World Heritage List", namely: Qin Shihuang's Mausoleum and Terra-cotta Warriors and Horses, Giant Wild Goose Pagoda, Little Wild Goose Pagoda, Daming Palace Ruins of Tang Dynasty, Weiyang Palace Ruins in Chang'an City, and Xingjiao Temple Tower. Xi'an is an inexhaustible history book and an endless cultural course. As a world historical and cultural city, Xi'an's historical culture, Silk Road culture, flourishing culture, red culture, fashion culture, etc. all demonstrate the most enduring cultural confidence of the Chinese nation and bring soul into Xi'an's MICE industry. Xi'an is rich in cultural tourism resources and has outstanding advantages. In the construction of "The Belt and Road Initiative", it has huge development potential, and it is a hot spot for investment.

◎规模化的会展产业 /Large-Scale Conference and Exhibition Industry

西安近年来不断培育、整合国内外资源，提升会展规模和质量，使其尽快成长为具有国际化影响力的会展城市。依托高新区为引领的科创大走廊，办好全球硬科技创新大会，借助丝绸之路国际电影节、西安国际马拉松赛、丝路大学等一批国际化的平台，深化与"一带一路"沿线国家和地区的文化交流和旅游合作。2019 欧亚经济论坛、世界西商大会、丝绸之路国际旅游博览会、全球硬科技创新大会等在西安成功举办，进一步彰显陕西作为会奖目的地的极佳优势。

In recent years, Xi'an has continuously nurtured and integrated domestic and foreign resources to enhance the scale and quality of conferences and exhibitions, so that it can

grow into a conference and exhibition city with international influence as soon as possible. Relying on the high-tech zone as the leading science and technology corridor, holding the Global Hard Technology Innovation Conference, with the help of a number of international platforms such as the Silk Road International Film Festival, Xi'an International Marathon, and Silk Road University, it will deepen cultural exchanges and tourism cooperation with countries and regions along "the Belt and Road". 2019 Euro-Asia Economic Forum, the World Western Business Conference, the Silk Road International Tourism Expo, and the Global Hard Technology Innovation Conference have been successfully held in Xi'an, further demonstrating Shaanxi's excellent advantages as a MICE destination.

◎西安电子、半导体产业集群 /Xi'an Electronics and Semiconductor Industry Cluster

近年来，随着美光、华为、三星、中兴等一批行业龙头企业在陕西投资落地，有力带动了陕西的半导体企业从原来的六七十家增长到现在的两百多家，从单体项目到产业集群，龙头企业的辐射带动效应正在显现。西安的电子信息、半导体和航空航天业在国内非常发达，吸引了诸多国际会议、会展集中在西安举办交流，由此带给西安的影响不仅是这些贵宾来这个城市访问，还把当地的产业同国际接轨，对整个产业的发展具有重大意义。

In recent years, as a number of industry leading companies such as Micron, Huawei, Samsung, and ZTE have invested in Shaanxi, it has effectively driven the growth of Shaanxi's semiconductor companies from the original sixty or seventy to more than two hundred now. From monomer projects to industrial clusters, the radiation effects of leading enterprises are emerging. The electronic information, semiconductor, and aerospace industries in Xi'an are very developed in China, attracting many international conferences and exhibitions to be held here. The impact on Xi'an is not only those VIPs visiting this city, but also able to bring the local industry in line with international standards. It is of great significance to the development of the entire industry.

2.6 中国南京概况
An Overview of Nanjing, China

中国南京

南京是江苏省省会、特大城市、南京都市圈核心城市。南京是全国重要的科研教育基地和综合交通枢纽，下辖 11 个市辖区和 1 个国家级新区（江北新区），总面积 6,587.02 平方千米，2020 年底常住人口 931 万人。

Nanjing is the capital of Jiangsu Province, a mega-city, and the core city of Nanjing metropolitan area. It is an important scientific research and education base, and a comprehensive transportation hub in the country. It has 11 municipal jurisdictions and 1 national new district (Jiangbei New District), with a total area of 6,587.02 square kilometers, and a permanent population of 9.31 million by the end of 2020.

2. 6. 1 气候 /Climate

南京位于长江下游的中心地带。丘陵盆地为主，属亚热带季风气候。四季分明，雨水充沛。每年 6 月下旬到 7 月上旬为梅雨季节。南京春秋短、冬夏长，冬夏温差显著。

Nanjing is located in the center of the lower reaches of the Yangtze River. It is dominated by hilly basins and has a subtropical monsoon climate. It has four distinct seasons and abundant rain. Every year from late June to early July is the rainy season. Nanjing has short spring and autumn, and long winter and summer, and the temperature difference between winter and summer is significant.

2.6.2 交通 /Transportation

南京禄口国际机场，4F 级机场，是国家主要干线机场、一类航空口岸，与上海虹桥国际机场、上海浦东国际机场互为备降机场，有 2 条 3,600 米跑道、2 座航站楼，拥有 135 条国内航线和 23 条国际航线。南京铁路、地铁、轻轨、有轨电车等轨道交通的快速发展为城市的会奖旅游业发展提供了快捷、高效、大容量的客运交通支持。

Nanjing Lukou International Airport, 4F-class airport, is a major national trunk airport, and an A-type aviation port. Shanghai Hongqiao International Airport and Shanghai Pudong International Airport are its alternate airports and vice versa. There are two 3,600-meter runways, two terminals, 135 domestic routes and 23 international routes. The rapid development of Nanjing railway, subway, light rail, tram, etc. provides rapid, efficient, and large-capacity passenger transportation support for the development of the city's MICE industry.

2.6.3 展馆与酒店 /Exhibition Venues and Hotels

南京国际展览中心拥有 2,200 个国际标准展位。南京国际博览中心位于奥体，拥有 6,000 个国际标准展位，是 2013 年南京亚青会、2014 年南京青奥会比赛场馆，2018 年成为 UFI 国际认证展馆。南京集齐全球东方文华、阿布扎比瑞吉、柏悦等九大顶级酒店，共有五星级及以上酒店 21 家，四星级酒店 215 家，可满足不同层次的会奖团队需求。

Nanjing International Exhibition Center has 2,200 international standard booths. Nanjing International Expo Center (NIEC) is in the Olympic Sports Center with more than 6,000 international standard booths. NIEC is for 2013 Nanjing Youth Asian Games and 2014 Nanjing Youth Olympic Games. NIEC became a UFI international certification venue in 2018. Nanjing gathers nine top hotels such as Mandarin Oriental, Regal Abu Dhabi, Park Hyatt. There are 21 five-star and above hotels and 215 four-star hotels to meet the needs of different levels of the MICE team.

2.6.4 会奖目的地优势 /Advantages of MICE Destination

2018 年南京正式成为 ICCA 的成员。2019 年 1 月，南京市入选"2018 年 WFBA 世界特色魅力城市 200 强"榜单。南京曾成功举办"G20 财长会议""中美城市经济合作和投资会议""世博会南京主题论坛"等规模大、层次高、国际影响力强的国际性高端会议。2016 年至 2019 年南京共承办 ICCA 认证的国际会议 80 个。

In 2018, Nanjing officially became a member of ICCA. In January 2019, Nanjing was listed in "Top 200 WFBA Cities with World Characteristics and Charm in 2018". Nanjing has successfully held international high-end conferences with large scale, high-level, and great international influence, such as "G20 Finance Ministers Meeting" "Sino US Urban Economic Cooperation and Investment Conference" "World Expo Nanjing Theme Forum". From 2016 to 2019, Nanjing hosted 80 international conferences on ICCA certification.

◎特色旅游资源 /Unique Tourism Resources

南京素有"六朝佳丽地、金陵帝王州"的美誉，建城已有 2,400 多年。久负盛名的秦淮河上演着一代又一代风花雪月的故事。庄严肃穆的中山陵融合中国古代与西方建筑之精华，缅怀世纪伟人。世界文化遗产明孝陵代表了明初建筑和石刻艺术的最高成就。侵华日军南京大屠杀遇难同胞纪念馆，30 万受害者，每一个遇难者都有不可触碰的名字，每一个生还者都有不忍提及的往事。南京有着历史的厚重感与沧桑感，正因为有着一次次的生死考验，才使得南京历久弥新，焕发出更加灿烂的光彩。

Nanjing is known as the "Beauty of the Six Dynasties and the Emperor State". The city has been built for more than 2,400 years. The prestigious Qinhuaihe River staged stories from generation to generation. The majestic Dr. Sun Yat-sen's blends the essence of ancient Chinese and Western architecture, remembering the great man of the century. The World Cultural Heritage Ming Emperors Tomb represents the highest achievement of the architecture and stone carving arts of early Ming Dynasty. The Memorial Hall of the Victims in Nanjing Massacre by Japanese Invaders remembers 300,000 victims.

Each victim has an untouchable name; each survivor has a past that he/she can't bear to mention. Nanjing has a heavy sense of history and vicissitudes. It is because of the history of bearing life and death tests that makes Nanjing last for a long time and glow more brilliantly.

◎崇文重教、地杰人灵 /Advocating Culture and Education

南京崇文重教、名人辈出，享有"东南第一学"的美誉。南京高校众多，对外来人才极具包容性。南京在"中国最具人才吸引力城市 100 强"中排名第六，在吸引海归人才方面全国排名第七。历史名人众多，近 300 位较为有名，如祖冲之、曹雪芹、吴敬梓、陶行知等。南京的国家级非物质文化遗产有 145 种，如南京云锦、南京白局、秦淮灯会、南京剪纸等。南京云锦和昆曲被列入世界非物质文化遗产名录，讲述着中国匠人匠心传承的故事。南京申报了世界图书之都、网络文学之都，并打造了世界知名城市"南京周""双城记"等一批文化交流品牌。南京森林音乐会、南京文化艺术节等助推其国际会奖目的地城市的建设。

Nanjing advocates culture and education with many celebrities here. Therefore, it enjoys the reputation of "First Education City in the Southeast". Nanjing has many universities and is very inclusive of foreign talents. Nanjing ranks sixth among the "Top 100 Cities of Attracting Talents in China" and ranks seventh in attracting overseas returnees. There are many celebrities in history with nearly 300 of high reputation, such as Zu Chongzhi, Cao Xueqin, Wu Jingzi, and Tao Xingzhi. There are 145 kinds of national intangible cultural heritage in Nanjing, such as Nanjing Brocade, Nanjing Baiju, Qinhuai Lantern Festival, Nanjing Paper-cutting. Nanjing Brocade and Kun Opera are included in the list of World Intangible Cultural Heritage, telling the story of Chinese craftsmen's ingenuity. Nanjing declared the world's book capital and online literature capital, and built several cultural exchange brands such as the world-famous "Nanjing Week" and "A Tale of Two Cities". The Nanjing Forest Concert, Nanjing Culture and Arts Festival, etc. have boosted the construction of international MICE destination city.

◎ "一核三区" 新格局 /The New Pattern of "One Core, Three Areas"

南京 2020 年已初步形成 "一核三区" 的会展城市新格局：以国际博览中心为核心，江北新区、南京综合保税区与禄口空港、南部新城等区同步推进。建设中的溧水空港会展小镇，总投资约 80 亿元，将建成建筑面积 50 万平方米的滨水生态会展综合体。南京一年中举办大型展览 280 多个。

In 2020, Nanjing has initially formed a new pattern of "One core, Three Areas" for conference and exhibition: the International Expo Center is the core, with three areas of Jiangbei New Area, Nanjing Comprehensive Bonded Area and Lukou Airport, Southern New City advancing simultaneously. Lishui Airport Conference and Exhibition Town is under construction, with a total investment of about 8 billion yuan. It will become a waterfront ecological exhibition complex with a construction area of 500,000 square meters. Nanjing holds more than 280 large-scale exhibitions throughout the year.

2.7 中国深圳概况
An Overview of Shenzhen, China

深圳地处中国华南地区，是广东省副省级城市、超大城市，国务院批复确定的中国经济特区。截至 2019 年底，全市下辖 9 个行政区和 1 个新区，总面积 1,997.47 平方千米，常住人口 1,343.88 万人。

Shenzhen is in South China, a sub-provincial city and a mega-city in Guangdong Province, and a Special Economic Zone approved by the State Council. By the end of 2019, Shenzhen has 9 districts and 1 new district under its jurisdiction, with a total area of 1,997.47 square kilometers and a permanent population of 13.4388 million people.

2.7.1 气候 /Climate

深圳属南亚热带季风气候，长夏短冬。气候温和，日照充足，雨量充沛，年平均气温 23℃。春季天气多变，夏季长达 6 个多月。秋冬季节天气干燥少雨，冬季短暂、雨水稀少。

Shenzhen has a south subtropical monsoon climate, with long summer and short winter. The climate is mild, with plenty of sunshine and abundant rainfall, and the annual average temperature is 23℃. The weather in spring is changeable, and the summer is more than 6 months. The autumn and winter seasons are dry and lack of rain, and the winter is short with little rain.

2.7.2 交通 /Transportation

深圳宝安国际机场，4F 级民用机场，位于深圳市宝安区、珠江口东岸，距离深圳市区 32 千米，为国际枢纽机场，中国十二大干线机场之一、中国四大航空货运中心及快件集散中心之一及世界百强机场之一。2018 年，深圳宝安国际机场获"世界十大美丽机场"桂冠。深圳地铁目前已开通 8 条运营线路，有 17 条地铁同步在建。到 2035 年，深圳将建成超过 1,300 千米的轨道交通，覆盖全市各个区域。广深港高铁及以广州、深圳为中心的铁路网络格局加速深圳与粤港澳大湾区其他城市的融合。

Shenzhen Bao'an International Airport, a 4F-class civil airport, is located in Bao'an District, on the east bank of the Pearl River Estuary, 32 kilometers away from city area. It is an international hub, one of China's 12 major trunk airports, one of the four largest air cargo and express mail distribution centers in China, and one of the world's top 100 airports as well. In 2018, Shenzhen Bao'an International Airport won the title of "Top Ten Beautiful Airports in the World". The Shenzhen Metro has opened 8 operating lines, and 17 subways are under construction at the same time. By 2035, Shenzhen will build more than 1,300 kilometers of rail transit, covering all areas of the city. Guangzhou-Shenzhen-Hong Kong high-speed rail and Guangzhou-Shenzhen-centric railway network pattern accelerate the integration of Shenzhen and other cities in the Guangdong-Hong Kong-Macao Greater Bay Area.

2.7.3 展馆与酒店 /Exhibition Venues and Hotels

深圳国际会展中心占地总面积约 148 万平方米，二期建成后室内展览总面积达 50 万平方米，将成为全球最大的会展中心，紧邻深圳宝安国际机场。深圳中亚会展中心、深圳国际展览中心、深圳国际贸易中心、深圳会展中心等都是有口皆碑的展览中心。深圳共有五星级酒店 67 家。

The Shenzhen World Exhibition & Convention Center covers a total area of about 1.48 million square meters. After the completion of the second phase, the total area of the indoor exhibition will reach 500,000 square meters. It will become the world's largest exhibition center, close to Shenzhen Bao'an International Airport. Shenzhen Central Asia Convention and Exhibition Center, Shenzhen International Exhibition Center, Shenzhen International Trade Center, Shenzhen Convention and Exhibition Center, etc. are all well-known exhibition centers. There are 67 five-star hotels in Shenzhen.

2.7.4　会奖目的地优势 /Advantages of MICE Destination

深圳会奖市场极具发展优势，特别是其休闲度假领域，资源极为丰富，包括了高尔夫、俱乐部、温泉、沙滩、主题乐园、拓展营地等等。深圳优美的环境、良好的基础设施和独特的人文文化为会奖旅游业的快速发展创造了条件。2016年至 2019 年深圳承办 ICCA 认证的国际会议共 64 个。

Shenzhen MICE market has great development advantages, especially in the field of leisure and vacation. It has abundant resources, including golf, clubs, hot springs, beaches, theme parks, expansion camps, etc. Shenzhen's beautiful environment, good infrastructure, and unique culture have created conditions for the rapid development of MICE industry. From 2016 to 2019, Shenzhen hosted 64 international conferences on ICCA certification.

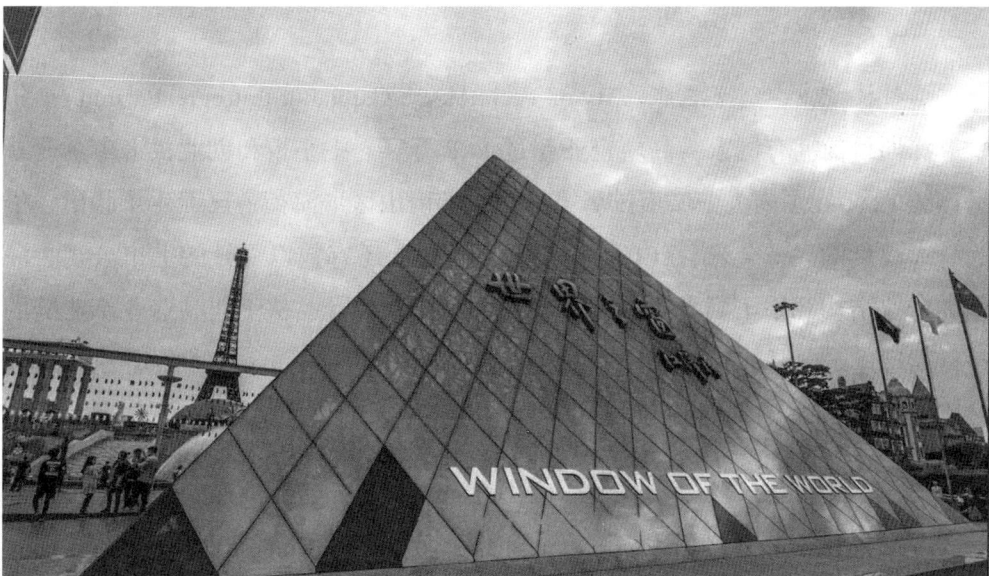

◎特色旅游资源/Unique Tourism Resources

深圳的旅游资源和娱乐设施独具特色：拥有世界最大的风景微缩区——锦绣中华、世界之窗，主题公园欢乐谷，还有大梅沙、南澳等海滩、海滨浴场。世界之窗公园分为世界广场、亚洲区、大洋洲区、欧洲区、非洲区、美洲区、世界雕塑园和国际街八大区域，含130多个景点。欢乐谷荣膺亚太十大主题公园，成为中国主题公园行业的领跑者。深圳西冲拥有长达4.5千米的沙滩海滨浴场、无敌海景，以及绝佳的地缘优势，这些使西冲成为深圳最大的露营基地，吸引众多游人来这里狂欢烧烤、办篝火晚会、沙滩漫步、观海上日出。

Shenzhen's tourism resources and entertainment facilities are unique: the world's largest scenic miniature area—Splendid China and Window of the World, Happy Valley theme park, as well as beaches such as Dameisha and Nanao. Window of the World Park is divided into eight major areas of World Plaza, Asia, Oceania, Europe, Africa, America, World Sculpture Garden, and International Street, including more than 130 attractions. Happy Valley is one of the top ten theme parks in Asia-Pacific, and the leader in China's theme park industry. Having nearly 4.5 kilometers of beaches, invincible sea views, and excellent geographical advantages, Shenzhen Xichong is the largest camping base in Shenzhen, attracting visitors with carnival barbecue, campfire party, beach walk, and watching the sunrise at sea.

◎科技之城、创业之都/City of Technology, Capital of Entrepreneurship

深圳目前拥有国家级高新企业超过1.12万家。中小板和创业板上市企业总量连续12年在国内大中城市排名第一。深圳南山区粤海街道已诞生了腾讯、华为、大疆、中兴、金蝶、TCL等科创巨头公司，还有数以百计的上市公司。深圳的产业结构几乎不到十年就有一次重大转型升级，已从工业制造业产业链的最低端迅速走向了数字革命时代的最前端。在5G的竞争中，深圳企业已抢占到技术专利的制高点，将和世界顶级企业一较高下。

Shenzhen currently has more than 11,200 state-level high-tech enterprises. The total number of SME and GEM listed companies has ranked first in domestic large and medium-sized cities for 12 consecutive years. Science and technology giants such as Tencent, Huawei, DJI, ZTE, Kingdee, TCL, and hundreds of other listed companies have been born on Yuehai Street, Nanshan District, Shenzhen. Shenzhen's industrial structure has undergone a major transformation and upgrading in less than a decade. It has rapidly moved from the lowest end of the industrial manufacturing industry chain to the forefront of the digital revolution era. In the competition of 5G, Shenzhen enterprises have seized the commanding heights of technology patents, and will compete with the world's top enterprises.

◎电子信息、人工智能领跑全国 /Electronic Information and Artificial Intelligence Leading the Country

深圳电子信息行业的优势明显，电子信息制造业产值占全国 1/6 份额。深圳是产业链最完整、资源配置最齐全的城市。只要提到 IT 硬件，任何一个配件都可以在几个小时之内找到供货企业，而在某些城市则需要一两周时间。新兴的 5G、物联网、新能源汽车电子、可穿戴设备、智慧城市等领域都为城市的发展带来了无限的机遇和空间。深圳已经形成人工智能产业化发展优势，跻身全国第三，产业聚焦效应日益凸显。以深圳湾科技生态园区为例，深圳湾科技生态园区是深圳市人工智能产业链专业园区，也是广东省首批人工智能产业园。

Shenzhen's electronic information industry has obvious advantages. The output value of the electronic information manufacturing industry accounts for one sixth of the national share. Shenzhen is the city with the most complete industrial chain and the most comprehensive resources. Regarding IT hardware, the supply company of any accessory can be found within a few hours. In some other cities, it takes a week or two. The emerging 5G, Internet of Things, new energy automotive electronics, wearable devices, smart cities, and other fields have brought unlimited opportunities and space for the development to the city. Shenzhen has formed an advantage in the development of industrialization of artificial intelligence and ranks third in the country. The industry focusing effect is becoming increasingly prominent. Taking Shenzhen Bay Science and Technology Ecological Park as an example, it is a professional park of AI industry chain and the first batch of AI industry parks in Guangdong Province.

2.8 中国广州概况
An Overview of Guangzhou, China

　　广州是广东省省会，是国家重要的中心城市、国际商贸中心和综合交通枢纽。总面积 7,434.40 平方千米，常住人口 1867.66 万人（2020 年）。广州地处中国南部，濒临南海，位于珠江三角洲北缘。

Being the capital of Guangdong Province, Guangzhou is an important central city, international trade center, and comprehensive transportation hub of China. The total area is 7,434.40 square kilometers, with a permanent population of 18.6766 million in 2020. Guangzhou is in southern China, bordering the South China Sea, and on the northern edge of the Pearl River Delta.

2.8.1 气候 /Climate

　　广州地处亚热带沿海，北回归线从中南部穿过，属海洋性亚热带季风气候，以温暖多雨、光热充足、夏季长、霜期短为特征。全年水热同期，雨量充沛，利于植物生长，为四季常绿、花团锦簇的"花城"。

Guangzhou is located on the subtropical coast and the Tropic of Cancer passes through the south-central part. It belongs to the maritime subtropical monsoon climate, being warm and rainy, having sufficient light and heat, with long summer and short frost period. The rain comes with heat all year round and the rainfall is abundant, which is conducive to the growth of plants. It is a "flower city" with evergreen view in four seasons.

2.8.2 交通 /Transportation

广州白云国际机场，4F 级民用国际机场，距广州市中心约 28 千米，是中国三大门户复合枢纽机场之一。广州有 7 座火车站，其中广州南站是全球最大的高铁 + 城轨交通枢纽。广州还是重要的出入境口岸，广州为部分国家人员提供 144 小时过境免签政策。广州的交通四通八达，出行十分便利。

Guangzhou Baiyun International Airport, a 4F-class civil international airport, is 28 kilometers away from city center and it is one of the three major gateway compound hubs in China. There are 7 railway stations in Guangzhou, of which Guangzhou South Railway Station is the world's largest high-speed rail + urban rail transportation hub. Guangzhou is also an important immigrant port of entry and exit. It provides 144-hour visa-free transit policies for personnel from some countries. The transportation is highly convenient.

2.8.3 展馆与酒店 /Exhibition Venues and Hotels

广州是中国最早的会展之都，拥有中国进出口商品交易会展馆、广州白云国际会议中心等国际一流水平的会展载体，以及支持会展业发展的政策体系。广州的酒店和服务业一直走在全国前列。目前广州国际会展中心（琶洲展馆）展馆总建筑面积 110 万平方米，琶洲成为高端酒店的另一个聚集点。

Guangzhou is the earliest convention and exhibition capital in China, with world-class exhibition carriers such as China Import and Export Fair Complex, Guangzhou Baiyun International Convention Center, and a policy system to support the development of the exhibition industry. Guangzhou's hotel and service industries have always been at the forefront of the country. At present, the total construction area of the Guangzhou International Convention and Exhibition Center (Pazhou Pavilion) is 1.1 million square meters. And Pazhou has become another focus area for luxurious hotels.

2.8.4 会奖目的地优势 /Advantages of MICE Destination

按照国家"十三五"规划对会展产业的规划，广州将打造与国际全面接轨的会、展、奖发展大格局，把广州的琶洲岛建设成为"世界第一会展城"，引领广州建设国际"会展＋旅游"产业中心城市。2016—2019 年广州共承办 ICCA 认证的国际会议 75 个（2016 年 26 个，2017 年 12 个，2018 年 20 个，2019 年 17 个）。

According to the national "Thirteenth Five-Year" plan for the convention and exhibition industry, Guangzhou will create a comprehensive development of conventions, exhibitions, and incentives that are in line with the international standard, and build Pazhou Island into "the world's first exhibition city", leading Guangzhou to become an international "exhibition + tourism" industrial center city. 75 ICCA certified international conferences were held in Guangzhou from 2016 to 2019 (26 in 2016, 12 in 2017, 20 in 2018, 17 in 2019).

◎特色旅游资源 /Unique Tourism Resources

广州既有滨海旅游资源，又有温泉、乡村旅游资源；广州长隆系列主题公园排在全球主题公园前列，每年吸引大量游客；深厚的广府文化、美食文化、中医养生文化等共同构成了独特的人文旅游资源。广州是广府文化的辐射中心，从公元 3 世纪起成为海上丝绸之路的主港，是世界唯一的 2,000 多年来长盛不衰的大港。

Guangzhou has coastal tourism resources, as well as hot springs and rural tourism resources. Guangzhou ChimeLong series of theme parks rank in the forefront of global theme parks, attracting a large number of tourists every year. The profound Cantonese culture, gourmet culture, traditional Chinese medicine health culture, etc. together form the unique humanistic tourism resources of Guangzhou. Guangzhou is the radiant center of Cantonese culture. It has been the major port of the Maritime Silk Road since the third century. And it is the only major port in the world that has lasted for more than 2,000 years.

◎千年商都 /Millennium Business Capital

广州，素以商业和贸易发达见称，有"千年商都"的名号，印证了其自古以来的商贸繁华。广州创办了国内第一家购物中心——天河城、国内第一家超市——友谊商店。广州跨境电商全国第一。广州商贸创新底蕴深厚，改革开放以来又以新模式、新业态发展，在多个领域走在全国前列。广州具有发展会奖旅游的优势基础。

Guangzhou, known for its well-developed business and commerce, enjoys the name of "Millennium Business Capital", witnessing his prosperous business since ancient times. Guangzhou established the first shopping center in China—Tianhe City and the first supermarket—Friendship Store. The cross-border e-commerce industry of Guangzhou ranks first nationally. Having a profound culture of business innovation, Guangzhou has been developing new business models since the reform and opening, and has been at the forefront in many fields. Guangzhou has the basis and advantages to develop MICE tourism.

◎广交会 /Canton Fair

广州拥有国内第一个具有全球影响的展览——广交会。每年春秋两季的广交会已经成为广州举办时间最长、影响力最大的展会之一。广交会的存在对广州酒店业的发展影响尤为明显。有数据显示，部分酒店在广交会期间的交易甚至创造约全年 1/4 的营业收入。广交会 2017《财富》全球论坛、2018 年世界航线发展大会、2019 世界港口大会、2019 年第六届中国会展会奖产业交易会等大型会议向世界展示了广州的新气象、新成就、新活力。

Guangzhou has the first domestic exhibition with global influence—China Import and Export Fair (Canton Fair). The every spring and autumn Canton Fair has become one of the longest and most influential exhibitions held in Guangzhou. The Canton Fair has a particularly obvious impact on the development of Guangzhou hotel industry. Statistics show that some hotels' transactions during the Canton Fair even generated about a quarter of operating income throughout the year. Major events like Canton Fair 2017 *Fortune Global Forum*, 2018 World Route Development Conference, 2019 World Ports Conference, 2019 6th China Exhibition (MICE) Industry Fair, etc. showed the world Guangzhou's new scene, new achievements, and new vitality.

2.9 中国厦门概况
An Overview of Xiamen, China

厦门地处福建省东南端，是福建省副省级城市、计划单列市。厦门是国务院批复确定的中国经济特区，也是国家综合配套改革试验区、自由贸易试验区。截至 2020 年底，全市下辖 6 个区，总面积 1,700.61 平方千米，常住人口 518 万人。2020 年，厦门被中华人民共和国住房和城乡建设部命名为国家生态园林城市。

Located in the southeastern tip of Fujian Province, Xiamen is a sub-provincial city and an individually planned city in the province. It is a Special Economic Zone approved by the State Council, a national comprehensive reform pilot zone and free trade pilot zone. By the end of 2020, the city has 6 districts with a total area of 1,700.61 square kilometers and a permanent population of 5.18 million. In 2020, it was named the National Ecological Garden City by the Ministry of Housing and Urban-Rural Development of People's Republic of China.

2.9.1　气候 /Climate

厦门地形以滨海平原、台地和丘陵为主。厦门属于亚热带海洋性季风气候，温和多雨，年平均气温在 21℃左右，夏无酷暑，冬无严寒。不过夏季易受台风侵袭，多集中在 7—9 月份。

The terrain of Xiamen is dominated by coastal plains, terraces, and hills. Xiamen has a subtropical maritime monsoon climate, mild and rainy, with an annual average temperature of about 21℃, without extreme temperatures in summer nor winter. However, it is susceptible to typhoons in summer, mostly in July to September.

2.9.2 交通 /Transportation

厦门高崎国际机场，4E 级机场，三面临海，位于厦门市厦门岛东北端，距市中心 10 千米，是长三角与珠三角之间最重要的国际航空枢纽。厦门翔安国际机场在建中，预计 2023 年通航，将取代厦门高崎国际机场。2020 年厦门已拥有 2 条地铁线：1 号线、2 号线，4 条地铁在建。厦门公交线路多、涉及面广，且 58.7% 的在营公交为新能源公交。

Xiamen Gaoqi International Airport, a 4E-class airport, facing the sea on three sides, is located at the northeast end of Xiamen Island in Xiamen City, 10 kilometers from city center. It is the most important international aviation hub between the Yangtze River Delta and the Pearl River Delta. Xiamen Xiang'an International Airport is under construction and expected to open in 2023. It will replace Xiamen Gaoqi International Airport. In 2020, Xiamen already has 2 subway lines: Line 1, Line 2, and 4 subways are under construction. Xiamen has many bus lines and extensive coverage, and 58.7% of the buses in operation are new energy buses.

2.9.3 展馆与酒店 /Exhibition Venues and Hotels

厦门国际会议展览中心由主场馆、厦门国际会展酒店、厦门国际会议中心、厦门海峡大剧院四部分组成。厦门国际会议展览中心主场馆及会展酒店占地面积 47 万平方米，总建筑面积 42 万平方米，是厦门市的标志性建筑之一。厦门五星级及以上酒店达 40 家。

Xiamen International Conference and Exhibition Center consists of four parts: the main venue, Xiamen International Conference and Exhibition Hotel, Xiamen International Conference Center, and Xiamen Straits Grand Theater. The main venue and the hotel together covers an area of 470,000 square meters, with a total construction area of 420,000 square meters, which is one of Xiamen's landmarks. There are 40 hotels with five stars and above in Xiamen.

2.9.4　会奖目的地优势 /Advantages of MICE Destination

厦门是国内较早推动会奖旅游业发展的城市之一，曾获"2017 中国最佳会奖营销目的地"。2020 年厦门文广体育有限公司成功加入 ICCA，将争取引进更多的国际体育赛事或者活动展会落地厦门。2019 年厦门市举办展览 236 场，2016 年至 2019 年厦门共承办 ICCA 认证的国际会议 38 个。

Xiamen is one of the earliest cities in China to promote the development of MICE industry, and has won the title of "2017 China's Best MICE Marketing Destination". In 2020, Xiamen Culture Media Sports Co., Ltd. successfully joined ICCA, striving to introduce more international sports events or exhibitions to Xiamen. In 2019, 236 exhibitions were held in Xiamen, and 38 ICCA international conferences were held in Xiamen from 2016 to 2019.

◎特色旅游资源 /Unique Tourism Resources

厦门拥有独特的旅游资源，如鼓浪屿、环岛路、南普陀寺、厦门大学，以及侨乡文化、军事文化、建筑风格等。大型国际水秀"海沧湖水秀"结合高科技手段和舞美等艺术形式，美丽绝伦，繁华胜景令人叹为观止。厦门的建筑既有浓郁的地方特色，又有厚重的文化底蕴。鼓浪屿的欧陆建筑和厦门的骑楼体现了异域建筑的光彩；红砖民房、"嘉庚风格"的建筑则蕴藏着博大精深的中华文化。集美大学、厦门大学则是"嘉庚风格"建筑的代表。厦门大学被称作中国最美大学，全球最美大学排名第九。

Xiamen enjoys the unique tourism resources such as Gulangyu Island, Huandao Road, Nanputuo Temple, Xiamen University, and overseas Chinese culture, military culture, architectural style. The large-scale water show "Haicang Lake Water Show" combined with high-tech methods and dance art forms, extremely beautiful and magnificent. Xiamen's architecture has both strong local characteristics and rich cultural heritage. Gulangyu's European-continental architecture and Xiamen's arcades reflect the

brilliance of exotic style; red brick houses and "Jiageng style" buildings contain profound Chinese culture. Jimei University and Xiamen University are the representatives of the "Jiageng style" architecture. Xiamen University is known as the most beautiful university in China, and the ninth most beautiful university in the world.

◎金砖国家峰会的效应 /The Effect of BRICS Summit

2017 年金砖国家峰会在厦门举办。这场国际盛会既为"厦门会晤"的举办创造了条件，又为会奖旅游业的发展提供了良好的环境。后峰会时代的厦门以更开放的姿态拥抱世界，打造别样精彩的世界名城；厦门的企业与金砖国家交往更加密切；厦门的会奖旅游业也因"金砖效应"大放异彩。

The 2017 BRICS Summit was held in Xiamen. This international event not only created the conditions for the "Xiamen Meeting", but also provided a good environment for the development of the MICE industry. In the post-summit era, Xiamen embraces the world with a more open posture and creates a different kind of wonderful world-class city. Xiamen's enterprises have closer communications with the BRICS countries. Its MICE industry also has a blooming development because of the "BRICS effect".

◎生态环境独特、民俗风情浓厚/Unique Ecological Environment and Strong Folk Customs

厦门素有"海上花园"美誉。城在海上,海在城中。走在厦门,每一步都是风景,高颜值的生态环境使它荣获"中国优秀旅游城市""国际花园城市""联合国人居奖"等称号。在这个国际港口旅游城市,既可以欣赏美丽迷人的海岛风光和感受现代化城市的无穷魅力,又可以领略独具特色的民俗风情。在厦门,古典与现代相交汇,民俗与典雅相融合。

Xiamen is known as the "Garden on the Sea". The city is on the sea, and the sea is in the city. Taking every step in Xiamen is a moment to enjoy scenery. Xiamen is awarded as "China's Outstanding Tourism City", "International Garden City", "United Nations Habitat Award", and other titles for its high-value ecological environment. In this international port and tourist city, you can not only enjoy the beautiful island scenery and feel the infinite charm of modern city, but also enjoy the unique folk customs. Xiamen enjoys a fusion of classic and modern, and of folk and elegance.

2.10 中国青岛概况
An Overview of Qingdao, China

青岛是山东省副省级城市、国务院批复确定的中国沿海重要中心城市、滨海度假旅游城市及国际性港口城市。截至 2020 年 11 月 1 日，全市总面积为 11,293 平方千米，常住人口 1,007.17 万人。青岛地处中国华东地区、山东半岛东南，东濒黄海，是"一带一路"的主要节点。

Qingdao is a vice-provincial city of Shandong Province, a State Council approved important central city along the coast of China, a coastal resort and tourism city, and an international port city. By November 1, 2020, with a total area of 11,293 square kilometers and a permanent population of 10,071,700, Qingdao is in the East China region, southeast of Shandong Peninsula, and east to the Yellow Sea. It is the main node of the Belt and Road.

2.10.1 气候 /Climate

青岛地处北温带季风区域，属温带季风气候。市区由于海洋环境的直接调节，受东南季风及海流、水团的影响，又具有显著的海洋性气候特点。空气湿润，雨量充沛，温度适中，四季分明。

Qingdao is in the north temperate monsoon region and has a temperate monsoon climate. The urban area is directly regulated by the marine environment and affected by the southeast monsoon, ocean currents, and water masses, so it has significant maritime climate characteristics. The air is humid, the rainfall is abundant, the temperature is moderate, and the four seasons are distinct.

2.10.2 交通 /Transportation

青岛流亭国际机场，4E 级民用国际机场，距青岛市中心约 23 千米，为中国十二大干线机场之一。德国文艺复兴风格的青岛站是胶济线沿途的中小车站，距海岸线仅 300 米，距今有 120 年的历史。

Qingdao Liuting International Airport, a 4E-class civil international airport, is about 23 kilometers away from city center and is one of China's 12 major trunk airport. The German Renaissance-style Qingdao Station is a small-to-medium-sized station along the Jiaoji Line. It is only 300 meters from the coastline and has a history of 120 years.

2.10.3 展馆与酒店 /Exhibition Venues and Hotels

受益于上合峰会效应，青岛的展馆和会议酒店等硬件设施得到了极大完善，会奖旅游业服务水平也显著提升。青岛国际会议中心、青岛国际会展中心、中铁青岛世博城、青岛国际博览中心、奥帆中心成为名副其实的"城市会客厅"。近几年青岛相继引进了洲际、喜达屋、凯悦、凯宾斯基、雅高、万达文创等 30 多个国内外知名品牌，为会奖旅游业的快速发展提供了强大后劲。青岛国际会议中心成功申请成为 ICCA 2020 年首批会员。

Benefiting from the SCO Summit effect, Qingdao's hardware facilities such as exhibition halls and conference hotels have been greatly improved, and the service level of the MICE industry has been significantly raised. Qingdao International Conference Center, Qingdao International Convention and Exhibition Center, China Railway Qingdao World Expo City, Qingdao International Expo Center, and Olympic Sailing Center have become veritable "urban parlors" of Qingdao. In recent years, Qingdao has introduced more than 30 well-known hotel brands, such as InterContinental, Starwood, Hyatt, Kempinski, Accor, and Wanda Cultural, providing a strong stamina for the rapid development of MICE industry. Qingdao International Convention Center successfully became the first batch of ICCA members in 2020.

2.10.4　会奖目的地优势 /Advantages of MICE Destination

会议买家团对 2019 年国内会奖活动目的地选择排名中，青岛列第 9 位，与杭州、厦门等同类副省级城市还存在一定差距。青岛曾获"2017 中国最具品牌价值会奖目的地""2018 中国领军智慧城市""2018 中国最具竞争力国际会奖目的地"等荣誉称号。

Qingdao ranks the 9th in the choice of MICE destinations in 2019 by the conference buyer group, which still has a certain gap with Hangzhou, Xiamen and other similar sub provincial cities. Qingdao has won the honorary titles of "2017 China's Most Famous Brand MICE Destination" "2018 China's Leading Intelligent City" "2018 China's Most Competitive International MICE Destination".

◎特色旅游资源 /Unique Tourism Resources

青岛作为国际知名滨海旅游度假胜地和国家历史文化名城，不但拥有我国沙质最细、面积最大、风景最美的号称"亚洲第一滩"的金沙滩，还拥有中国海岸线的第一高峰崂山。青岛的崂山道教文化、养生文化对海外游客具有相当大的吸引力，青岛城市的"德式风情"也是独一无二的，这些都成为青岛打造会奖目的地的独特旅游资源。

Qingdao, as an internationally well-known coastal tourist resort and a national historical and cultural city, not only has the "Asian First Beach" golden beach with China's finest sand, the largest area, and the most beautiful scenery, but also has the highest peak in China's coastline, Laoshan. Qingdao's Taoist culture and health culture of Laoshan Mountain are quite attractive to foreign tourists. The "German style" of Qingdao is also unique. These have become unique tourism resources for Qingdao to create a MICE destination.

◎会奖产业链日臻完善 /MICE Industry Improving Day by Day

青岛市政府大力推进会奖旅游业，为青岛打造国际一流的滨海度假旅游胜地提供了详细的发展路径。以"上合青岛峰会"为契机，以会带展、以展促会，与城市品牌互动、助力青岛成为国际知名会奖旅游目的地城市。2016 年至 2019 年青岛共承办 ICCA 认证的国际会议 38 个。

Qingdao municipal government has vigorously promoted MICE industry and provided a detailed development path for Qingdao to become an international first-class coastal resort. Taking the opportunity of the "Shanghai Cooperation Qingdao Summit", it will guide the exhibition, promote exhibition, expand the city brand, and help Qingdao become a famous international MICE destination. During the four years from 2016 to 2019, Qingdao hosted 38 international conferences on ICCA certification.

◎国际化色彩浓厚 /Strong Globalization

青岛既有世界知名的工业品牌，如百年青啤，又有海尔、海信等国际化程度较高的知名企业。国际啤酒节、音乐节、电影节、海洋节、克利伯帆船赛、国际时装周、青岛金沙滩文化旅游节、海之情旅游节等国际节庆活动的举办，进一步扩大了城市的知名度和影响力。

Qingdao has world-renowned industrial brands, such as Centennial Qingdao Beer, as well as Haier and Hisense. Hosting international festivals such as International Beer Festival, Music Festival, Film Festival, Ocean Festival, Clipper Regatta, International Fashion Week, Qingdao Golden Beach Cultural Tourism Festival, Haizhiqing Tourism Festival has further improved the city's popularity and influence.

3 中国境外会奖目的地城市
MICE Destination Cities Outside China

3.1 法国巴黎概况
An Overview of Paris, France

法国巴黎

巴黎是法兰西共和国的首都和最大的城市，世界 5 个国际大都市之一（其余 4 个分别为纽约、伦敦、东京、香港），被 GaWC 评为 Alpha+ 级世界一线城市。巴黎位于法国北部巴黎盆地的中央，横跨塞纳河两岸。广义的巴黎有小巴黎和大巴黎之分。小巴黎即巴黎市区，面积 105.4 平方千米，人口 218 万（2021年 7 月）。大巴黎还包括市区周围的 7 个省，共同组成大巴黎都会区。大巴黎都会区人口约为 1,100 万，占据全国人口的 1/6。截至 2016 年，巴黎一共被划分为20 个区（第 1 区以罗浮宫为中心，以顺时针排列命名）。

Paris is the capital, the largest city of the French Republic, and one of the five international metropolises in the world (the remaining four are New York, London, Tokyo, and Hong Kong). It is rated as an Alpha+ World First-tier city by GaWC. Paris is located in the center of the Paris Basin in northern France, across the banks of Seine River. Broadly speaking, there are small Paris and great Paris. Small Paris is the urban area of Paris, with an area of 105.4 square kilometers and a population of 2.24 million (July 2021). Great Paris includes seven provinces around the urban area, which together form the Great Paris metropolitan area. The metropolitan area of Paris has a population of approximately 11 million, accounting for one sixth of the country's population. By 2016, Paris was divided into 20 districts (the 1st district is centered on the Louvre Museum, namely clockwise).

3.1.1 气候 /Climate

巴黎属于温和的海洋性气候，夏无酷暑，冬无严寒。全年降雨分布均衡。

Paris has a mild maritime climate, with no extreme heat in summer nor severe cold in winter. Rainfall distribution is balanced throughout the year.

3.1.2 交通 /Transportation

巴黎一共有 3 个机场，其中夏尔·戴高乐国际机场，也被称为鲁瓦西机场，是欧洲第二大中转平台，仅次于伦敦的希斯罗机场，是世界重要的机场之一。法国巴黎市区内共有 7 座火车站，巴黎北站已成为欧洲最重要的火车站之一。地铁连接其他几大车站，旅客可经由四通八达的地铁，迅速抵达巴黎各地。

There are three airports in Paris, of which Charles de Gaulle International Airport, also known as Roissy Airport is the second largest transit platform in Europe and one of the most important airports in the world, only second to London Heathrow Airport. There are seven railway stations in Paris. Among them, Paris North Railway Station has become one of the most important railway stations in Europe. Several other major stations are connected by metros. Passengers can quickly reach all parts of Paris through the metros in all directions.

3.1.3 展馆与酒店 /Exhibitions Venues and Hotels

巴黎拥有 15 个展览中心，3 个最大的展览馆分别为巴黎展览中心、维勒班特展览中心和布尔日展览中心。巴黎展览业主要由巴黎展览协会、巴黎工商会等五大协会负责。巴黎的酒店具有多重面貌，既有极尽奢华的顶级酒店，又有设计感十足的生态酒店，为游客创造了丰富独特的住宿体验。

Paris has fifteen exhibition centers and the three largest exhibition centers are Paris Exhibition Center, Villepinte Exhibition Center, and Bourges Exhibition Center. The Paris exhibition industry is mainly in charge of five major associations including Paris Exhibition Association and Paris Chamber of Commerce and Industry. The hotels in Paris have multiple features, including extremely luxurious top hotels and eco-hotels with full sense of design, creating a rich and unique accommodation experience for tourists.

3.1.4 会奖目的地优势 /Advantages of MICE Destination

法国每年约举办 1,500 个展览。巴黎拥有约 60 万平方米的展览面积，每年举办展会的数量约占全法国的 70%。展会不仅为展览公司、场馆和展览服务公司带来收益，也带动了相关行业的发展，每年为巴黎创造约 55 亿欧元经济效益。2018 年巴黎再次成为世界会展之都。据 ICCA 发布的"2019 年 ICCA 会议城市排名"，巴黎以举办 237 个会议位居全球第一。

France holds about 1,500 exhibitions every year. Paris has an exhibition area of about 600,000 square meters. The number of exhibitions held annually accounts for about 70% of the total in France. The exhibition not only brings benefits to exhibition companies, venues, and exhibition service companies, but also drives the development of related industries. The exhibition generates about 5.5 billion euros in economic benefits every year for Paris. Paris became the world's convention and exhibition capital again in 2018. According to the "2019 ICCA Conference Cities Ranking" released by ICCA, Paris ranked first in the world with 237 conferences.

◎特色旅游资源 /Unique Tourism Resources

浪漫之都巴黎是世界第一大旅游目的地，其对游客的吸引力是其他城市无法匹敌的。整座城市就像一部流动的电影，她若不动人，世间再无浪漫。充满风情的塞纳河把巴黎一分为二：赋予右岸以现代与繁华，而把气质与优雅留给左岸。

众多博物馆、美术馆让巴黎成为世界艺术殿堂。罗浮宫、巴黎歌剧院、凡尔赛宫、蓬皮杜中心、奥赛博物馆等各种类型的博物馆 300 多个。罗浮宫博物馆作为世界四大博物馆之首，珍藏 40 余万件艺术珍品，《断臂维纳斯》《胜利女神像》《蒙娜丽莎》为罗浮宫的 3 件镇馆之宝。巴黎的艺术瑰宝让每一位到访者流连忘返。

The romantic capital of Paris is the world's first tourist destination, and its attraction to tourists is unmatched by other cities. The whole city is like a running movie. If she was not charming, there would be no romance in the world. The elegant Seine River divides Paris in two: giving the right bank modernity and prosperity, while leaving temperament and elegance to the left bank.

The numerous museums and art galleries make Paris a palace of world art. There are more than 300 museums and galleries of various types, such as the Louvre Museum, Paris Opera, Versailles, the Pompidou Center, Orsay Museum. As the first of the four major museums in the world, the Louvre Museum has a collection of more than 400,000 art treasures. *Venus de Milo*, *Victoire de Samothrace*, and *Mona Lisa* are the three treasures of the Louvre Museum. The art treasures of Paris make every visitor linger.

◎巴黎车展 /Paris Auto Show

巴黎车展起源于 1898 年，是世界上第一个车展，与法兰克福车展、日内瓦

国际汽车展、北美车展和东京车展并称为五大车展。巴黎的车展如同时装，总能给人争奇斗艳的感觉。每年一届，1976 年开始，巴黎车展与德国法兰克福车展交替举办，成为欧洲大陆第二大的汽车展览会。参展人数、记者数和观众数达百万，给巴黎带来了惊人的收入。

Originated in 1898, Paris Auto Show is the world's first auto show. It is one of the five major auto shows together with Frankfurt Auto Show, Geneva International Auto Show, North American Auto Show, and Tokyo Auto Show. Paris Auto Show is like fashion, always giving people the feeling of fascination. Once a year, starting in 1976, Paris Auto Show and Frankfurt Motor Show in Germany were alternately held. The former became the second largest automobile exhibition in continental Europe. Millions of exhibitors, journalists, and visitors bring Paris amazing income.

◎巴黎时装周 /Paris Fashion Week
巴黎时装周起源于 1910 年，由法国时装协会主办，协会的最高宗旨是将巴黎作为世界时装之都的地位打造得坚如磐石。巴黎吸纳了全世界的时装精英。殿堂级时装设计师们几乎每一个都是通过巴黎进入世界的视野。纽约展示商业，米兰展示技艺，伦敦展示胆色，唯有巴黎展示梦想。

Originated in 1910, Paris Fashion Week is sponsored by the French Fashion Association. The highest aim of the association is to build Paris as a rock as the world's fashion capital. Paris has absorbed fashion elites from all over the world. Almost every one of the top fashion designers has entered the world's vision through Paris. New York shows business, Milan shows craftmanship, London shows courage, only Paris shows dreams.

3.2 奥地利维也纳概况
An Overview of Vienna, Austria

维也纳位于多瑙河畔，是奥地利的首都和最大的城市，被誉为"世界音乐之都"。维也纳拥有超过 191.1 万（2021 年 1 月 1 日）的人口，共由 23 个区组成。维也纳以多瑙河为界又分为内城、外城和郊区 3 个部分。维也纳的居民主要分布于维也纳的西部和东部。

Located on the Danube River, Vienna is the capital and the largest city of Austria, known as the "World Capital of Classical Music". Vienna has a population of more than 1.911 million (Jan. 1, 2021) and is composed of 23 districts. Vienna is divided into three parts: inner city, outer city, and suburbs, with the Danube as the boundary. The residents of Vienna are mainly distributed in the west and east of Vienna.

3.2.1 气候/Climate

维也纳的气候为温带海洋性气候。维也纳的降水量很小，干旱期较长，冬季较其他奥地利城市温暖。一年约有 60 天是夏天，70 天是冰冻期，天气寒冷异常。

Vienna has a temperate maritime climate. The precipitation is very small, the dry period is long, and the winter is warmer than that in other Austrian cities. About 60 days a year are summer and 70 days are freezing periods with cold and abnormal weather.

3.2.2 交通 /Transportation

维也纳国际机场也称施威夏特机场，位于奥地利维也纳东南方 18 千米（11 英里）处，是全国最繁忙和最大的机场。维也纳最主要的火车站有两座：中央火车站和西火车站，中央火车站是维也纳最大的火车站。

Vienna International Airport, also known as Schwechat Airport, is located 18 kilometers (11 miles) southeast of Vienna, and is the busiest and largest airport in the country. There are two main railway stations in Vienna: Central Railway Station and West Railway Station. Central Railway Station is the largest railway station in Vienna.

3.2.3 展馆与酒店 /Exhibition Venues and Hotels

维也纳展览及会议中心建于 2004 年，凭借着可变形的展馆及会议室，能够满足展会组织者的各种需求。建筑群总面积约为 19 万平方米，由 4 座主建筑组成。会议大厦共有 9 个会议大厅，可同时容纳 4,000 人办公和 1,600 人开会，设有英、法、汉、西、俄、阿等 9 种语言的同声传译室，以及电子计算中心、银行、商店等附属设施。在新建筑落成之后，原来分散在维也纳市的联合国机构都集中于此。维也纳酒店业一直以高品质服务为准则，以客户满意度为唯一检验标准，在消费者中收获了极高的口碑评价。

Vienna Exhibition and Conference Center was built in 2004. With its deformable exhibition halls and meeting rooms, it can meet the various needs of exhibition organizers. The total area of the building complex is about 190,000 square meters and it consists of 4 main buildings. In the conference building, there are 9 conference halls, which can accommodate 4,000 people for office and 1,600 people for meetings at the same time. It has simultaneous interpretation rooms in 9 languages including English, French, Chinese, Spanish, Russian, and Arabic, and affiliated facilities such as an electronic computing center, banks, and shops. After the completion of the new building, the United Nations agencies that were originally scattered in Vienna are concentrated here. The hotel industry in Vienna has always taken high-quality service as the criterion and customer satisfaction as the only test standard, and has gained a very high reputation among consumers.

3.2.4　会奖目的地优势 /Advantages of MICE Destination

每年来维也纳参加各种国际会议的外国代表有 2 万多人次。2018 年维也纳共举办了 172 个 ICCA 认证的国际会议，2019 年 149 个，在 2019 年全球宜居城市及智能城市指数排名中均位列第一。ICCA 认为，维也纳是全球第二大最受欢迎的会奖活动举办地。

More than 20,000 foreign representatives come to Vienna to participate in various international conferences every year. In 2018, Vienna hosted 172 ICCA-certified international conferences, and 149 in 2019, ranking first both in the 2019 Global Livable Cities and Smart Cities Index. ICCA believes that Vienna is the world's second most popular city for MICE activities.

◎特色旅游资源 /Unique Tourism Resources

维也纳是欧洲古典音乐的摇篮。奥地利历史上有众多名扬世界的音乐家，如海顿、莫扎特、舒伯特、约翰·施特劳斯，还有出生于德国但长期在奥地利生活的贝多芬等。在两个多世纪里，这些音乐大师为奥地利留下了极其丰厚的文化遗产，形成了其独特的民族传统文化。维也纳也因此登上了文化巅峰，被誉为"世界音乐之都"。维也纳拥有世界上最豪华的国家歌剧院、闻名遐迩的音乐大厅和第一流水平的交响乐团。每年1月1日在维也纳金色大厅举行的新年音乐会，奥地利总统和维也纳各界名流都要出席。世界各地著名的音乐家也经常在金色大厅演出，他们的精彩表演吸引着成千上万的国内外观众。

Vienna is the cradle of European classical music. There are many famous musicians in Austrian history, including Haydn, Mozart, Schubert, John Strauss, and Beethoven who was born in Germany but lived in Austria for a long time. For more than two centuries, these music masters had left Austria with an extremely rich cultural heritage and formed its unique traditional culture. Vienna has thus reached the cultural peak and is known as the "Music Capital of the World". Vienna has the most luxurious Vienna State Opera, the famous concert hall, and the first-class Symphony Orchestra. The new year's concert is held in the Golden Hall of Vienna on January 1 every year, attended by the Austrian president and the celebrities from all walks of life in Vienna. Famous musicians from all over the world often perform in the Golden Hall of Vienna. Their wonderful performances attract thousands of audiences at home and abroad.

◎世界最宜居城市/The Most Livable City in the World

维也纳是一座欧洲历史名城，文化古迹众多。它有一种兼容并蓄的气度，已经连续多年被联合国人居署评为全球最宜居的城市之一。行走在维也纳的街头，建筑和大自然融合在一起，原生态的环境让人倍感恬淡安逸。中心古城区为世界遗产，著名景点有蓝色的多瑙河、维也纳森林、阿尔贝蒂娜博物馆、斯蒂芬大教堂、霍夫堡皇宫、美泉宫、维也纳艺术史博物馆、金色大厅等。

Vienna is a historical European city with many cultural monuments. It has an inclusive attitude and has been rated as one of the most livable cities in the world by UN-Habitat for many years. Walking on the streets of Vienna, architecture and nature blend together, and the original ecological environment makes people feel calm and comfortable. The Old Town in the center is a World Heritage Site. Famous attractions include the Blue Danube, Vienna Woods, Albertina Museum, Stephansdom, Hofburg Palace, Schönbrunn Palace, Vienna Art History Museum, Golden Hall, etc.

◎联合国总部/United Nations Headquarters

维也纳是联合国的4个官方驻地之一（其他3个为纽约、日内瓦、内罗华），也是石油输出国组织、欧洲安全与合作组织和国际原子能机构的总部，以及其他国际机构的所在地。

Vienna is one of the four official locations of the United Nations (the other three are New York, Geneva, and Nairobi), as well as the location of headquarters of OPEC—Organization of Petroleum Exporting Countries, OSCE—Organization for Security and Cooperation in Europe, IAEA—International Atomic Energy Agency, and other international agencies.

3.3 英国伦敦概况
An Overview of London, UK

伦敦是大不列颠及北爱尔兰联合王国首都，世界第一大金融中心。伦敦和纽约并列为全世界最顶级的国际大都会。大伦敦都会区被划分为伦敦市和周围的 32 个自治市。伦敦市人口约为 900 万（2020 年），大伦敦都会区人口约 1,400 万（2020 年）。大伦敦都会区又可划分为伦敦城、西伦敦、东伦敦和南伦敦 4 个区域。

London, the world's largest financial center, is the capital of the United Kingdom of Great Britain and Northern Ireland. London and New York are ranked as the world's top international metropolises. The Greater London Metropolitan Area is divided into the City of London and its surrounding 32 municipalities. The City of London has a population of 9 million (2020), and the Greater London Metropolitan Area has a population of approximately 14 million (2020). The Greater London Metropolitan Area can be divided into four regions: London City, West London, East London, and South London.

3.3.1 气候 /Climate

伦敦受北大西洋暖流和西风影响，属温带海洋性气候，四季温差小。夏季凉爽，冬季温暖。空气湿润，多雨雾，秋冬尤甚。在伦敦冬季有罕见结冰的情况。

Affected by the North Atlantic warm current and west winds, London has a temperate maritime climate, and the temperature difference between four seasons is small. The summer is cool, and the winter is warm. The air is humid, while rainy and foggy days are very common especially in autumn and winter. Icing conditions are rare in winter in London.

3.3.2 交通 /Transportation

伦敦一共有 6 个机场，最大的机场为伦敦希思罗国际机场，距离市区大约 24 千米，是伦敦最大、最繁忙的机场。其他 5 个是伦敦城市机场、盖特威克机场、斯坦斯特德机场、卢顿机场和伦敦绍森德机场。伦敦作为全英的交通枢纽，铁路系统四通八达，10 座火车站遍布整个伦敦。

There are 6 airports in London. The largest and busiest airport is London Heathrow International Airport, about 24 kilometers from the city center. The other 5 are London City Airport, Gatwick Airport, Stansted Airport, Luton Airport, and London Southend Airport. As a transportation hub in the UK, London has an extensive railway system and 10 railway stations throughout London.

3.3.3 展馆与酒店 /Exhibition Venues and Hotels

伦敦有 11 家会展中心，展览总面积达 900 万平方米。伦敦 Excel 国际会展中心（ExCel LONDON）又称伦敦展览会议中心，位于伦敦皇家码头的中心，是伦敦最大、最重要的展览中心之一。2012 年伦敦的奥运会和残奥会、现场设计大展和最高档现场汽车论坛都在此举行。据专家估算，展览中心的市场价值达 5.6 亿英镑。

伦敦有 150 多家会议酒店，既有奢华的老牌酒店，以高度个性化的服务和对细节孜孜不倦的追求成为名流的不二选择，又有浸没式的精品酒店，精巧随性。两类酒店可以满足客人的不同需求。

There are 11 convention and exhibition centers in London with a total exhibition area of 9 million square meters. ExCel LONDON, also known as the London Exhibition and Conference Center, is located in the center of London's Royal Docks, and is one of the largest and most important exhibition centers in London. 2012 London Olympic Games and Paralympic Games, Grand Designs Live, and top gear live car forum were held here. According to expert estimation, the market value of the exhibition center amounts to 560 million pounds.

There are more than 150 conference hotels in London. With highly personalized service and tireless pursuit of details, luxurious and old hotels have become the best choice for celebrities, and there are also immersive boutique hotels which are exquisite and casual. Both can satisfy different needs of the guests.

3.3.4　会奖目的地优势 /Advantages of MICE Destination

伦敦会展业呈现高度国际化、专业化的特点。英国每年超过 30% 的展会都是在伦敦举办，伦敦会展直接收入高达 20 多亿英镑。2019 年伦敦举办 ICCA 认证的国际会议 143 个，位居全球第 8 位。2019 年全球城市潜力排名，伦敦位居榜首。

The London convention and exhibition industry is characterized by a high degree of internationalization and specialization. More than 30% of the exhibitions in the UK are held in London each year, and the direct revenue of London conventions and exhibitions is as high as more than 2 billion pounds. In 2019, London hosted 143 ICCA-certified international conferences, ranking eighth in the world. London ranked first in "2019 Global City Potential Rankings".

◎特色旅游资源 /Unique Tourism Resources

伦敦是将现代城市和古典文化融合得最好的城市之一。游弋于古典与现代之间，感受传统与创新的激烈碰撞，不同的种族、宗教和文化在这里交融，形成了独特的英伦文化。伦敦温文尔雅又个性十足，内敛矜持又前卫张狂，集古典的高贵与优雅、现代的时尚和尊荣于一身。伦敦具有丰富的教育资源，是全球最佳留学城市之一。根据 2018 QS 世界大学排名，伦敦有 7 所大学进入前 100 名。排名第一的是剑桥大学，其次是牛津大学，然后为伦敦大学学院、帝国理工大学、伦敦政治经济学院及伦敦国王学院。

London is one of the cities where modern and ancient cultures blend best. Cruising between classical and modern, feeling the fierce collision of tradition and innovation, different races, religions, and cultures blending here, form a unique culture of diversity in London. London is gentle and full of personality, restrained and avant-garde, combining classic nobleness and elegance, modern fashion and honor. London has rich educational resources and has become one of the best cities to study abroad. According to the 2018 QS World University Rankings, London has 7 universities in the top 100. Cambridge University is ranked first, followed by Oxford University, and the rest are University College London, Imperial College London, The London School of Economics and Political Science, and King's College London.

◎世界第一大金融中心 /The World's Largest Financial Center

伦敦拥有多个世界第一：世界第一大金融中心、第一大财富中心，以及 2018 年被 GaWC 评为 Alpha+ 级世界一线城市第一名。据统计 2018 年有近 5,000 名超级富豪（资产净值超过 3,000 万美元）生活在伦敦。关键原因在于伦敦是全球顶级城市，具有"金融首都"的美称。它是全球投资者和居民满意度最高的城市，为全球超级富豪提供了巨大的发展机会，对他国居民也具有极大的吸引力。不断流入的人口为全球富豪的资产提供稳定的保值及升值后盾。

London has many world firsts: the world's largest financial center and the largest wealth center. In 2018, it ranked first in the world's first-tier cities in the Alpha+ class by GaWC. According to statistics, nearly 5,000 super-rich (with a net worth of more than US$30 million) lived in London in 2018. The key reason is that London is a top global city with the reputation of "Financial Capital". It is a global city with the highest satisfaction from global investors and residents. It provides huge development opportunities for the global super-rich, and it is also extremely attractive to residents of other countries. The constant influx of the population can provide a stable backing for the preservation and appreciation of the global wealthy's assets.

◎*世界顶级国际大都会* /The World's Top International Metropolis

伦敦具有极高的国际城市品牌价值。伦敦的博物馆、图书馆、电影院和体育场馆数量居世界首位。它是世界上唯一一个举办过 3 次奥运会的城市，拥有世界上最出名的电影节、音乐节、时装周。伦敦是国际贸易中心和国际港口城市。伦敦是高端制造业跨国控制中心，不少高端制造企业的总部或控制中心设在伦敦，有 19 家世界 500 强企业总部设在伦敦。伦敦金属交易所是世界上最大的金属交易所。伦敦的国际石油交易所及伦敦商品交易所在世界上的地位也举足轻重。

London has an extremely high brand value of international city. It has the largest number of museums, libraries, cinemas, and stadiums in the world. It is the only city that has hosted Olympic Games three times and has the most famous film festivals, music festivals, and fashion weeks in the world. London is an international trade center and international port city. London is a multinational control center for high-end manufacturing, and the headquarters or control centers of many high-end manufacturing companies are located in London. 19 Fortune 500 companies are headquartered in London. The London Metal Exchange is the world's largest metal exchange in the world. London's International Petroleum Exchange and London Commodity Exchange also play an important role in the world.

3.4 德国柏林概况
An Overview of Berlin, Germany

👥德国柏林

柏林位于德国东北部，是德国的首都和最大的城市，也是德国的政治、文化及经济中心。柏林人口约为 366.9 万（2020 年），全市共分为 12 个区。第二次世界大战后，城市被分为两个区域，即东柏林和西柏林。1990 年柏林墙推倒，两德统一。柏林重新获得了德国首都的地位，并驻有 147 个外国大使馆。在2019 年全球城市 500 强榜单中，柏林排名第 7。2023 年世界夏季特殊奥林匹克运动会将在柏林举行。

Located in the northeast of the country, Berlin is the capital, the largest city, and the political, cultural, economic center of Germany. It has a population of approximately 3.669 million (2020) with 12 districts. After the Second World War, the city was divided into two regions, that is East Berlin and West Berlin. In 1990, the Berlin Wall was overthrown and the two Germanys were reunified. Berlin regained the status of the German capital and had 147 foreign embassies. The city ranked seventh in the 2019 Global Top 500 Cities. The 2023 World Summer Special Olympics Games will be held in Berlin.

3.4.1 气候 /Climate

柏林是温和的大陆性气候，夏季炎热，冬季寒冷。夏季平均气温在 22℃和25℃之间，夏季最高气温大约为 30℃。

Berlin has a mild continental climate, with hot summer and cold winter. The average temperature in summer is between 22°C and 25°C, and the maximum temperature in summer is about 30°C.

3.4.2 交通 /Transportation

柏林有 3 个机场，但是目前在用的机场只有 2 个：泰格尔机场简称柏林机场，距离首都柏林市中心 8 千米，是柏林的主要国际机场；舍内菲尔德机场原为东柏林机场，位于柏林市中心东南部 18 千米处。柏林市区有地铁、城市快铁（似区间车）、有轨电车、公交等 4 种交通方式可选择。

There are three airports in Berlin, but only two are in use currently: Tegel Airport, known as Berlin Airport, 8 kilometers away from city center, is the main international airport of Berlin; Schoenfeld Airport was originally the East Berlin Airport, located 18 kilometers southeast of the city center. There are four modes of transportation in Berlin, including metro, urban express (like a shuttle bus), tram, and bus.

3.4.3 展馆与酒店 /Exhibition Venues and Hotels

德国作为世界上最大的博览会基地，品牌化、专业化的特点明显。德国柏林展览中心坐落于德国柏林夏洛腾堡区，是德国第五大展馆。展览中心室内展览总面积约为 19 万平方米，包括 27 个相连的展示厅。柏林拥有 800 多家现代化酒店和特色活动举办地，而且服务业水准一流。与其他欧洲国家相比，酒店价格具有极优的性价比。

As the largest exposition base in the world, Germany has obvious characteristics of branding and specialization. Located in the Charlottenburg district of Berlin, Messe Berlin is the fifth largest exhibition venue in Germany. The indoor exhibition area of the exhibition center is about 190,000 square meters, including 27 connecting exhibition halls. Berlin has more than 800 modern hotels and venues for special events, and the service industry is of first-class standard. Compared with other European countries, the hotel prices are extremely cost-effective.

3.4.4　会奖目的地优势 /Advantages of MICE Destination

根据 2019 年 ICCA 的全球会议城市数据，柏林共举办了 176 个会议，位居全球第 3 位。柏林不仅仅是个生机勃勃的创意之都，作为会议和活动举办地还为会奖旅游业树立了新的标杆。

According to data of the ICCA Global Conference Cities in 2019, Berlin held 176 conferences, ranking third in the world. Berlin is not only a vibrant creative city, but also a new benchmark for MICE industry as a venue for conferences and events.

◎特色旅游资源 /Unique Tourism Resources

在柏林你可以体验中西方文化的差异、历史与现代的冲突，以及严谨与活跃之间的碰撞。柏林随处可见的建筑都具有古老与现代的和谐之美。第二次世界大战遗留下来的残缺的教堂与时尚的购物中心交相辉映；百年建筑改建的精品酒店，让历史的厚重融合于轻度奢华之中；有着两百多年历史的皇家瓷器厂，经过精心"装扮"，每个细节都散发着强烈的现代气息；柏林墙遗址与柏林活动中心相邻而居，历史文化与现代活动互为促进。柏林是一首优美的时代变奏曲，对会奖旅游参与者而言将是一种难得的人生经历。

In Berlin you can experience differences between Chinese and Western cultures, conflicts between history and modernity, and collision between rigor and activity. The buildings everywhere in Berlin have the beauty of ancient and modern harmony: the church ruins left over the Second World War and the fashionable shopping malls complement each other; the royal porcelain factory with a history of over two hundred years has been carefully "dressed up", and every detail exudes a strong modern atmosphere; the ruins of the Berlin Wall are adjacent to the Berlin Event Center, promoting historical culture and modern activities together. Berlin is a beautiful variation of the times, which will be a rare life experience for MICE participants.

◎柏林展会个性突出 /Outstanding Characteristics of Berlin Exhibitions

柏林国际航空航天展览会每两年在德国首都柏林举办，已有百年历史，有静态展和飞行展，是国际上最大的航空航天专业展览之一。柏林国际旅游交易会（ITB）始办于 1966 年的西柏林，当时只有 5 个国家的 9 个展商参展。今天 ITB 已发展成为全球规模和影响力最大的旅游业综合性展会。ITB 被称作是整个旅游业的黄金市场，被誉为旅游业的"奥林匹克"。

The Berlin International Aerospace Exhibition is held in Capital Berlin every two years. It has a century of history and is one of the largest professional aerospace exhibitions in the world. It includes static exhibitions and flying exhibitions. ITB was founded in West Berlin in 1966 with only 9 exhibitors from 5 countries. Today, ITB has developed into a comprehensive tourism industry exhibition with the largest scale and influence in the world. ITB is called the golden market for tourism industry, and it is also honored the "Olympics" of tourism industry.

◎足球赛事成为国家盛事 /Football Events Become a National Event

足球是德国的国民运动。大型足球赛几乎等同于国家盛事。家家户户都会在窗外挂出大大的国旗。路上也会见到许多高歌欢呼或身穿黑、红、黄的球迷。身着国旗色的球迷聚集在布兰登堡门前，看着大型转播，为德国足球队加油！

Football is a national sport in Germany. Large-scale football matches are almost equal to a national event. Every family will hang a big national flag outside the window. You will also see many fans cheering on the road or wearing black, red, and yellow. Germany fans in the colors of the national flag gather in front of Brandenburg gate, watching the large-scale broadcast and cheering for the German football team!

3.5 日本东京概况
An Overview of Tokyo, Japan

东京面向东京湾，是日本首都及最大的城市。狭义上说的"东京"指东京都，广义上指东京都市圈。通常将东京都中心区域最主要的 6 个区——千代田区、中央区、港区、新宿区、文京区、台东区，并称为"都心 6 区"。东京人口数达 1,405 万（2021 年 7 月 1 日），东京都市圈的人口数则达 3,700 万，是全球规模最大的都会区之一，也是传统上全球四大世界级城市之一，被 GaWC 评 Alpha+ 级世界一线城市。

Facing Tokyo Bay, Tokyo is the capital of Japan and the largest city. "Tokyo" refers to Tokyo Metropolis in a narrow sense, and broadly refers to the Greater Tokyo Metropolitan Area. Six main districts in the central area of Tokyo—Chiyoda, Chuo, Minato, Shinjuku, Bunkyo, and Taito are called "6 downtown areas". Tokyo has a population of 14.05 million (July 1, 2021), and the Tokyo Metropolitan Area has a population of 37 million. It is one of the largest metropolitan areas in the world and one of the four largest world-class cities in the world. It is rated Alpha+ by GaWC first-tier cities in the world.

3.5.1　气候 /Climate

东京属于亚热带季风气候，四季分明，降水充沛。夏季受东南季风影响，降水较多，冬季则降雪较少。7 月底至 8 月底是全年之中阳光最多、天气最晴的时候。

Tokyo has a subtropical monsoon climate with four distinct seasons and abundant precipitation. Affected by the southeast monsoon, summer has much precipitation while winter has little snow. From late July to late August, this period enjoys most sunshine and finest weather in a year.

3.5.2　交通 /Transportation

东京拥有两座日本国家中心机场：东京羽田国际机场和东京成田国际机场。东京火车站是日本陆上交通的总枢纽，拥有 18 条 JR 线路、10 条新干线，以及东京地下铁 2 条线路，是最能代表日本繁忙交通的车站。东京的公共交通以电车和有轨电车为主，交通线路和车站十分密集，换乘也比较复杂，东京的交通堪称全球最精密的系统。

Tokyo has two national center airports: Tokyo Haneda International Airport and Tokyo Narita International Airport. Tokyo Railway Station is the general hub of land transportation in Japan. The railway station has 18 JR lines, 10 Shinkansen lines, and 2 subway lines in Tokyo. It is the most representative station for the heavy traffic in Japan. Tokyo's public transportation is dominated by trolleybus and trams. The transportation lines and stations are very dense, and the transfer is complicated. Tokyo's transportation can be called the most sophisticated system in the world.

3.5.3　展馆与酒店 /Exhibitions Venues and Hotels

东京有明国际展览中心是日本规模最大、技术最先进的展览中心，整个展览中心面积约 24.3 万平方米；其所在地是通过人工填海造成的，距离东京市中心很近，从东京站到国际展览中心只需要 20 分钟。幕张国际会展中心是日本第二大展览馆。它占地面积达 21 万平方米，建筑面积达 16 万平方米，展览面积达 7 万平方米，东京车展、东京电玩展、日本高新技术博览会等大型展会均在此举办。

日本不实行酒店星级评定制度，东京的住宿一般分为日式旅馆和酒店两大类。东京已成为仅次于纽约的高消费地区，豪华酒店单间价格每晚不少于 3,000 元人民币。东京住宿的高评价很大程度上源于其优质的服务。

Tokyo International Exhibition Center, Ariake, is Japan's largest and most advanced exhibition center. The entire exhibition center covers an area of about 243,000 square meters. Its location is created by artificial reclamation. It is very close to the center of Tokyo, only 20 minutes away from Tokyo Station. Makuhari International Exhibition Center is the second largest exhibition venue in Japan. It covers an area of 210,000 square meters, a construction area of 160,000 square meters, and an exhibition area of 70,000 square meters. Tokyo Motor Show, Tokyo Game Show, Japan Combined Exhibition of Advanced Techndogy (CEATEC Japan) and other large-scale exhibitions are held here.

Japan does not implement a star rating system for hotels. Accommodations in Tokyo are generally divided into two categories: Japanese hotels and hotels. Tokyo has become a high-consumption area second only to New York. The price of a single room in luxury hotels is no less than RMB 3,000 per night. The high evaluation of Tokyo accommodation is largely due to its excellent service.

3.5.4　会奖目的地优势 /Advantages of MICE Destination

东京是一座迷人的城市，既保留了日本传统文化的精髓，又充满了时尚活力与时代感。春秋两季就如东京最美的两件衣裳，春天赏樱，秋日观枫，最惬意不过。相扑、歌舞伎、能剧等传统技艺在东京有着举足轻重的地位。东京ICCA 认证的国际会议 2019 年 131 个，2018 年 123 个。东京荣获 "2018 年度十佳品质深度旅行目的地" 奖项。

Tokyo is a charming city, which not only retains the essence of Japanese traditional culture , but also is full of fashion vitality and sense of the times. Spring and autumn are just like the two most beautiful clothes in Tokyo. It's most pleasant to watch cherry trees in spring and maple trees in autumn. However, traditional skills such as sumo, kabuki, and Noh all play an important role in Tokyo. There are 131 international conferences certified by ICCA in Tokyo in 2019 and 123 in 2018. Tokyo won the award of "Top 10 Quality In-depth Travel Destinations in 2018".

◎特色旅游资源 /Unique Tourism Resources

东京是全球最重要的经济和金融城市之一。东京是日本的经济中心，日本的主要公司都集中在这里。素有"东京心脏"之称的银座，是当地最繁华的商业区。东京综合实力评价为亚洲城市第一位，通常人们将其视为与伦敦、纽约、巴黎并列，具有主导性的全球四大城市之一。

Tokyo is one of the most important economic and financial cities in the world. Tokyo is the economic center of Japan and major Japanese companies are concentrated here. Ginza, known as the "Heart of Tokyo", is the most prosperous business district in the area. Tokyo's comprehensive strength is rated first in Asian cities. People generally regard it as one of the four leading global cities with dominance in parallel with London, New York, and Paris.

◎独具节制美和匠心精神的社会 /A Society with Unique Beauty and Ingenuity

日本是一个秩序社会，儒家思想与价值观对日本社会与文化产生了极大的影响。日本文化强调自律，强调在力所能及的范围内帮助别人，不制造麻烦。

这种文化深入每个国民的骨髓。匠心精神代表了技艺的传承，以及对每个环节、每道工序、每个细节都精工细作的严谨精神。在匠心精神的拉动下，不仅仅是传统的手工业，日本各行各业的背后，都有着一群把用户需求打磨到极致的制造者。细节文化的追求让"日本制造"成为了精品的代名词。

Japan is an orderly society. Confucian ideas and values have great influence on Japanese society and culture. Japanese culture emphasizes self-discipline, helping others within the limits of one's capabilities, not causing trouble. This culture penetrates the bones of every person. Japanese ingenuity represents the inheritance of craftsmanship, as well as a rigorous spirit of precision in every link, every process, and every detail. Driven by the spirit of ingenuity, not only traditional handicrafts, but behind all walks of life in Japan, there are a group of manufacturing that satisfies the users' needs to the extreme. The pursuit of details has made "Made in Japan" synonymous with fine products.

◎风靡全球的动漫 /Anime & Manga Conquer the World

日本漫画享有绝对的全球第一地位。日本是世界第一大动漫强国。日本的动漫作品是现实与主张的结合体，是客观现象与主观思想的轮回穿插，是用虚拟情节构建真实世界的艺术方式。热血、理想、哲思、讽刺……都被涵盖在动漫包罗万象的题材库中。漫画里随处可见逼真的个体美和各种鲜明特色的文化影子。在刀光剑影的市场竞争中一步步拼杀出来，日本动漫几乎个个是精彩绝伦的杰作。2016年，日本动漫已经占据国际市场60%的份额，在欧美市场的占有率更是达到了80%以上。

Japanese manga enjoys absolute first position in the world. Japan is the world's largest animation power. Japanese manga and anime works are a combination of reality and proposition, a reincarnation of objective phenomena and subjective thoughts, and an artistic way of constructing the real world with virtual plots. Enthusiasm, ideals, philosophies, satires and so on are all covered in the all-encompassing theme library of manga and anime. The realistic beauty and various cultural shadows with distinctive characteristics can be seen everywhere in manga. Struggling to stand out in the fierce market competition, almost all Japanese manga and anime are wonderful masterpieces. In 2016, Japanese manga and anime occupied 60% of the international market, and its share in the European and American markets reached more than 80%.

3.6 新加坡概况
An Overview of Singapore

新加坡毗邻马六甲海峡南口，与马来西亚紧邻。新加坡的土地面积是 719.1 平方千米，海岸线总长 200 余千米。全国由新加坡岛、圣淘沙、姐妹岛等 60 余个岛屿组成。新加坡是一个城邦国家，故无省市之分，而是以符合都市规划的方式将全国划分为 5 个社区（行政区）。新加坡人口总数 568.6 万（2021 年 8 月），其中常住人口 402.3 万，非常住人口 166.3 万。

Singapore is adjacent to the southern exit of the Strait of Malacca and close to Malaysia. Singapore has a land area of 719.1 square kilometers and a total coastline of more than 200 kilometers. The country is composed of more than 60 islands such as Singapore Island, Sentosa, and Sister Island. Singapore is a city-state country. So, there is no province or city. But the country is divided into five communities (administrative regions) in a way that is consistent with urban planning. The total population of Singapore is 5.686 million (August 2021), of which 4.023 million are permanent residents and 1.663 million are non-residents.

3.6.1　气候 /Climate

新加坡地处热带，长年受赤道低压带控制，为赤道多雨气候，年温差和日温差小。平均气温在 23℃至 34℃之间。11 月至次年 3 月左右为雨季，6 月到 9 月为旱季。4 月到 5 月和 10 月到 11 月为季风交替月，岛内的最高温度可以达到 35℃。

Singapore is in the tropics, controlled by the equatorial low-pressure zone all year round. It has a rainy climate in the equator. The annual temperature difference and the daily temperature difference are small. The average temperature is between 23 and 34°C. The rainy season is from November to next March, the dry season is from June to September, the monsoon is alternated from April to May and from October to November. The highest temperature on the island can reach 35°C.

3.6.2 交通 /Transportation

新加坡最著名的机场是樟宜国际机场，一共有 4 个航站楼，分别是 T1、T2、T3 及廉价航站楼。这座国际化枢纽机场的占地面积只有 13 平方千米，是北京大兴国际机场的 1/8，但它的吞吐量在 2018 年达到了 6,560 万人次，位列世界第七。这里是新加坡的国际门户，也是新加坡目前唯一的客运机场。这座机场风景优美，服务优良，连年被 Skytrax 评为"世界最佳机场"。

Singapore's most famous airport is Changi International Airport, which has four terminals, namely T1, T2, T3, and budget airline terminal. The international hub airport covers an area of only 13 square kilometers, which is one eighth of Beijing Daxing International Airport. But its throughput reached 65.6 million passengers in 2018, ranking seventh in the world. This is Singapore's international gateway and the only passenger airport in Singapore at present. This airport has beautiful scenery and excellent service. It was named "Best Airport in the World" by Skytrax in successive years.

3.6.3 展览与酒店 /Exhibitions Venues and Hotels

新加坡拥有丰富的酒店、场馆、景点和基础设施。新加坡博览中心、新加坡新达城国际展览与会议中心及莱佛士城会议中心是新加坡三大会展中心。新加坡博览中心是亚洲最大的展览馆，占地面积 250,000 平方米，该中心建有 60,000 平方米的展览馆。截至 2018 年底，新加坡拥有 67,000 个酒店房间，2023 年前预计再增长 2,823 间。新加坡的酒店业亚洲排名第一。

Singapore has a wealth of hotels, venues, attractions, and infrastructure. Singapore EXPO, Singapore Suntec Singapore Convention & Exhibition Center, and Raffles City Convention Center are the three major convention and exhibition centers in Singapore. Singapore Expo is the largest exhibition center in Asia, covering an area of 250,000 square meters, having an exhibition hall of 60,000 square meters. By the end of 2018, Singapore had 67,000 hotel rooms, and is expected to increase by 2,823 by 2023. Singapore's hotel industry ranks first in Asia.

3.6.4　会奖目的地优势 /Advantages of MICE Destination

新加坡每年举办大型会展活动近 4,000 个，展会规模和数量居亚洲第一位。彭博 2018 年创新经济论坛、2018 年全球青年科学家峰会等影响力巨大。2018 年举办 ICCA 认证的国际会议 145 个，2019 年 148 个，新加坡获评"2019 年度最佳海外会奖旅游目的地（短途）"和"世界最喜爱商务城市"。这两个称号代表了会奖旅游业对新加坡的高度认可。

Singapore holds nearly 4000 large-scale exhibitions every year, ranking first in Asia in terms of scale and quantity. Bloomberg's 2018 Innovation Economy Forum, 2018 Global Young Scientists Summit, etc. have great influence. There were 145 ICCA-certified international conferences held in 2018 and 148 in 2019. Singapore was awarded the "Best Overseas MICE Destinations (Short Distance) in 2019" and the "World's Favorite Business City". These two titles represent the high recognition of Singapore by the MICE industry.

◎特色旅游资源 /Unique Tourism Resources

新加坡被称作"花园城市"，城市绿化覆盖率达到 50%，不仅有室外绿化，还有室内绿化、屋顶绿化，甚至可见建筑外墙上的垂直绿化。温度全年维持在 25℃左右。位于市中心的新加坡植物园被评为世界自然遗产，成为"花园城市"的精华版。环球影城和全球最大的水族馆给这座不大的城市增添了无穷的魅力。

Singapore is called a "Garden City" with a 50% rate of urban green coverage. It not only has outdoor greening, but also indoor greening, roof greening, and even vertical greening on the exterior wall of the building. The temperature stays at about 25 degrees throughout the year. The Singapore Botanic Garden located in the city center is rated as a World Natural Heritage and has become the essence of the "Garden City". Universal Studios and the world's largest aquarium add infinite charm to this small city.

◎法律完善，投资环境宽松 /Well-Developed Legal System and Welcoming Investment Environment

新加坡是全球著名的国际金融中心，是全球资本的重要集散地之一。新加坡法律体系健全，政府高效廉洁；社会治安良好，是世界上犯罪率最低的国家之一；拥有天然深水避风海港和集装箱码头，以及全球最优质的机场。这些因素都能为外来投资提供快捷高效的服务和相对公平的投资环境。

Singapore is a world-renowned international financial center and one of the important distribution centers of global capital. Singapore has a sound legal system and a government with high efficiency and honesty. Singapore boosts a good social security and one of the lowest crime rates in the world. Singapore also owns natural deep-water sheltered seaports and container terminals as well as the world's best airport. All these factors can provide fast and efficient services and relatively fair investment environment for foreign investment.

◎ 引进人才，教育理念先进 /Introducing Talents and Advanced Education Concepts

新加坡的教育综合实力不容小觑。在 OECD 最新教育素质全球排名和国际 PISA 项目排名中，新加坡均名列榜首。对一个基本达到 100% 城市化，又是一个资源匮乏的国家来说，国际竞争靠什么？靠的是人才竞争，新加坡有很好的移民政策来引进人才。李光耀曾说："教育是确保下一代取得成功的最重要元素。"对新加坡人来说，不论种族、宗教或语言，让有天赋才能的年轻一代接受最好的教育，让孩子成为社会的精英是每个家庭的期待。政府一直努力把新加坡的每所学校都打造成名校，实施形式多样的公民教育，形成共同的价值观。

Singapore's comprehensive strength in education cannot be underestimated. Singapore ranks first in the OECD's latest global ranking of education quality and international PISA project rankings. For a country that has almost reached 100% urbanization and is also a resource-poor country, what does its international competition rely on? The answer is the talent. Singapore has a very good immigration policy to attract talent. Lee Kuan Yew once said "Education is the most important element to ensure the success of the next generation." For Singaporeans, regardless of race, religion or language, it is the expectation of every family to enable the gifted young generation to receive the best education and make their children the elites of society. The government has been working hard to make every school in Singapore prestigious, implementing various forms of civic education and forming common values.

西班牙巴塞罗那

3.7 西班牙巴塞罗那概况
An Overview of Barcelona, Spain

巴塞罗那是西班牙第二大城市，全市面积 101.9 平方千米。2020 年市区人口约 162 万，也是世界上人口最稠密的城市之一。巴塞罗那是一个港口城市，是西班牙最重要的贸易、工业和金融基地，也是享誉世界的地中海风光旅游目的地和世界著名的历史文化名城。

Barcelona is the second largest city in Spain, covering an area of 101.9 square kilometers. In 2020, the urban population is about 1.62 million, and it is also one of the most densely populated cities in the world. As a port city, Barcelona is the most important trade, industrial, and financial base of Spain. It is also a world-famous Mediterranean scenic destination and a world-famous historical and cultural city.

3.7.1 气候 /Climate

巴塞罗那位于西班牙东北部地中海沿岸，属地中海式气候，夏季炎热干旱，冬季温和多雨。冬天的平均温度为 11℃，夏天的平均气温为 24℃。

Barcelona is located in the Mediterranean coast of northeast Spain , with a Mediterranean climate. It is hot and dry in summer, but mild and rainy in winter. The average temperature is 11°C in winter and 24°C in summer.

3.7.2 交通 /Transportation

巴塞罗那机场位于巴塞罗纳市中心的西南方，距离市中心 13 千米。该机场是西班牙第二大机场，主要用于国内航线和飞往欧洲各个目的地，机场分 A、B、C 3 个航站楼，其中 A 航站楼是供国际航班的出发与抵达，从巴塞罗那飞往欧洲其他国家的距离较首都马德里更近，机票价格也更加便宜。巴塞罗那拥有干净、准时的地铁系统，有 2 个长途巴士站，大部分的车都是从北站发车。

Barcelona Airport is located in the southwest of Barcelona, 13 kilometers away from the city center. The airport is the second largest airport in Spain, which is mainly used for domestic routes and European destinations. The airport is divided into three terminals: A, B, and C. Terminal A is for the departure and arrival of international flights. Compared with capital city Madrid, it is closer and cheaper to fly from Barcelona to other European countries. Barcelona has a clean and punctual subway system, and two long-distance bus stations. Most buses depart from the North Station.

3.7.3 展馆与酒店 /Exhibitions Venues and Hotels

巴塞罗那国际会展中心是欧洲第二大的展览中心，整座会展中心的造型与设计理念都非常前卫，展览面积 24 万平方米，分布在 8 个现代化大型展馆中，同时另外建有 6 个总面积达 14,000 平方米、可容纳 3,000~12,000 位展会人员的会议中心。在巴塞罗那国际会展中心的四周分布着超过 4,900 间客房，最大程度满足了参展商与观展买家的需求。

Barcelona International Convention and Exhibition Center is the second largest exhibition center in Europe. The shape and design concept of the entire exhibition center are very avant-garde. The exhibition area is 240,000 square meters, which is distributed in eight modern large-scale exhibition halls. At the same time, it has 6 conference centers, which cover a total area of 14,000 square meters, and can accommodate 3,000—12,000 exhibitors. More than 4,900 rooms are distributed around the Barcelona International Convention and Exhibition Center, meeting the needs of exhibitors and buyers to the greatest extent.

3.7.4　会奖目的地优势 /Advantages of MICE Destination

1992 年第 25 届奥运会让巴塞罗那成了整个欧洲的第三大度假旅游胜地，来巴塞罗那的游客猛增，现在每年游客达 3,000 万人次。据 ICCA 发布的 "ICCA 会议城市排名"，2017 年巴塞罗那举办了 195 个（全球第一），2018 年 163 个，2019 举办 156 个（两年均为全球第四）。IBTM World 是全球旅游行业的领先展览，也是目前全球规模最大、知名度最高的会奖行业展会之一，每年 11 月或 12 月在巴塞罗那举办。

The 25th Olympic Games in 1992 made Barcelona the third largest holiday destination in Europe. The number of tourists to Barcelona has soared, and now there are 30 million tourists every year. According to the "ICCA Conference City Rankings" released by ICCA, Barcelona held 195 international meetings in 2017 (ranking first in

the world), 163 in 2018, and 156 in 2019 (both ranking fourth). IBTM World is a leading global exhibition and one of the largest well-known MICE industry exhibitions in the world. It is held in Barcelona in November or December every year.

◎特色旅游资源 /Unique Tourism Resources

巴塞罗那是伊比利亚半岛的一个海滨城市，一年 365 天，巴塞罗那至少有 300 天是晴天。温煦的海风、岸边游弋的鱼群、柔软的沙滩及在沙滩上热情似火享受日光浴的人们构成了一道洒脱和奔放的风景线。仅一条海滨人行道，便将城市的喧嚣隔绝在另一个世界。人们可以吹着海风，听着海滩边的酒吧音乐，吃一道西班牙地道的海鲜饭，享受地中海的阳光与海浪。同时，1992 年第 25 届巴塞罗那奥运会被公认为奥运史上的成功典范，给城市的持续发展注入了动力和活力，并带来了长期的积极影响。

Barcelona is a coastal city on the Iberian Peninsula with at least 300 sunny days in a year. The warm breeze blowing, the fish swimming on the shore, and the people sunbathing on the soft beach form a free and unrestrained landscape. Seaside sidewalk separates the hustle and bustle of the city in another world. People can blow the sea breeze, listen to the bar music on the beach, eat a typical Spanish paella, and fully enjoy the Mediterranean sunshine and waves. Meanwhile, the 25th Barcelona Olympic Games in 1992 has been recognized as a successful model in the Olympic history, which has generated power and vitality into the sustainable development of the city, and has brought a long-term positive impact.

◎艺术与天才之城 /City of Art and Genius

巴塞罗那是一座艺术与天才之城，上帝的灵魂不小心遗落在人间。毫不夸张地说，没有天才建筑师高迪就没有现在的巴塞罗那，他的 7 项建筑被列入世界文化遗产：奎尔公园（Parc Guell）、圭尔宫（Palau Guell）、米拉公寓（Casa Mila）、文森特公寓（Casa Vicens）、圣家族大教堂（Temple De La Sagrada Famelia）、巴布罗之家（Casa Batelle）和圭尔住宅区的地下教堂（Esglasia De La Colonia Guell）。他的作品把雕塑艺术与灵魂世界完美地结合在一起，创造了世界上独一无二的建筑作品。高迪是一个梦想家又是一个建筑家，他的作品无论从艺术审美的角度还是从文化价值的角度，都是历史上的一个奇迹，前无古人，后无来者。

Barcelona is a city of art and genius, where God left his soul and love on the earth. It is no exaggeration to say that without the talented architect Gaudi, there would be no Barcelona now. He has seven buildings on the World Cultural Heritage List. They are Parc Guell, Palau Guell, Casa Mila, Casa Vicens, Temple De La Sagrada Famelia, Casa Batelle, and Esglasia De La Colonia Guell. His works perfectly combine sculpture with the soul, creating the unique architectural works in the world. Gaudi is not only a dreamer but also an architect. His works are a miracle in history, no matter from the perspective of artistic aesthetics or from the perspective of cultural value. Gaudi created a record that has never been approached and will never be approached again.

◎足球俱乐部与天才球星 /Football Club and Talented Stars

巴塞罗那足球俱乐部（Fútbol Club Barcelona），简称巴萨（Barça），是西班牙足球甲级联赛传统豪门之一。球队主场诺坎普球场可容纳近 10 万名观众，是全欧洲最大及世界第二大的足球场。皇家马德里、巴塞罗那、国际米兰、AC 米兰和曼联等成为球迷心中五大顶级俱乐部，天才梅西及诺坎普球场成为巴塞罗那最闪亮的名片。除了梅西，巴萨历史上还出过小罗、马拉多纳、哈维等天才球星。

Fútbol Club Barcelona, or Barça for short, is one of the traditional giants of Spanish Football League. Camp Nou is the largest football field in Europe and the second largest in the world, with a capacity of nearly 100,000 spectators. Real Madrid, Barcelona, Inter Milan, AC Milan, and Manchester United have become the top five clubs for football fans, while talent Messi and Camp Nou stadium have become the most shining business cards of Barcelona. In addition to Messi, there also have been talented stars such as Ronaldinho, Maradona, Xavi in Barça's history.

3.8 捷克布拉格概况
An Overview of Prague, Czech Republic

布拉格是捷克共和国的首都和最大的城市。该市地处欧洲大陆的中心，与周边国家联系密切。布拉格为直辖市，人口131万（2020年），是全球第一个整座城市被指定为世界文化遗产的城市。

Prague is the capital and largest city of the Czech Republic. It is located in the center of the European continent and has close ties with neighboring countries. Prague is a municipality directly under the central government with a population of 1.31 million (2020). It is the first city in the world to be designated as a World Cultural Heritage.

3.8.1　气候 /Climate

布拉格属于温带大陆性气候，四季分明，受大陆气团控制，冬季长而寒冷，经常下雪；夏季比较短，阳光充足，天气炎热，全年少雨。

Prague belongs to temperate continental climate, with four distinct seasons. Controlled by continental air mass, winter is long and cold with much snow in Prague while summer is relatively short, sunny and hot, with little rain all year round.

3.8.2　交通 /Transportation

布拉格国际机场位于首都布拉格西北面，离市中心14千米，是捷克最大的民用机场，是捷克航空公司的总部基地。每年客流量大约为1,200万人次，是欧盟最繁忙的机场之一。布拉格拥有完整的公共交通系统，布拉格中央火车站是哈布斯帝国即将消亡时最辉煌的建筑之一，高高的穹顶和彩色玻璃窗仍扬溢着帝国的自信。

Prague International Airport is located in the northwest of the capital Prague, 14 kilometers away from the city center. It is the largest civil airport in Czech Republic and the headquarter of Czech Airlines. With an annual passenger flow of about 12 million, it is one of the busiest airports in European Union. Prague has a complete public transportation system. Prague Main Railway Station is one of the most brilliant buildings when Habsburg Empire was about to extinct. The high dome and colored glass windows still express the confidence of the Empire.

3.8.3 展馆与酒店 /Exhibitions Venues and Hotels

布拉格有众多适合举办会议的场所，可满足不同需求。整个捷克有 235 家服务会奖客人的酒店，都能够承办不同规模的会奖活动。布拉格有现代风格的时尚酒店，有古典浪漫的宫殿式酒店，也有宁静典雅的修道院酒店。因布拉格不在欧元区，平均消费不高，住宿餐饮是欧洲会奖目的地里性价比较高的城市。

Prague has many venues suitable for holding conferences, which can meet different needs. There are 235 hotels serving MICE guests in the Czech Republic, all of which can host MICE events of different scales. Prague has modern and fashionable hotels, classical and romantic palace hotels, and also has quiet and elegant monastery hotels. Because Prague is not in the euro zone, the average consumption is not high, whose accommodation and catering are relatively cost-effective among European MICE destinations.

3.8.4 会奖目的地优势 /Advantages of MICE Destination

布拉格是欧洲前十位的旅游城市，外国游客人数仅次于伦敦、巴黎、罗马、马德里和柏林。2019 年布拉格举办 ICCA 认证的国际会议 138 个，位居全球第九位。在布拉格，吸引游客的不只有布拉格之春国际音乐节，布拉格之秋国际音乐节、布拉格国际木偶节、布拉格"假日世界"国际旅游博览会等文化活动也吸引着大量游客的目光。

Prague is one of the top ten tourism cities in Europe. The number of foreign tourists is second only to London, Paris, Rome, Madrid, and Berlin. In 2019, Prague held 138 ICCA-certified international conferences, ranking ninth in the world. In Prague, not only the Prague Spring International Music Festival, Prague Autumn International Music Festival, Prague International Puppet Festival, Prague "Holiday World" International Tourism Expo, and other cultural activities also attract a large number of tourists.

◎特色旅游资源/Unique Tourism Resources

布拉格拥有 900 多年的历史，是世界上唯一一个整座城市被列为世界文化遗产的城市。置身于这座古城，感觉进入一个童话的世界：布拉格城堡、圣维特大教堂、查理大桥、老城广场、天文钟，你会本能地忘记时间，迷失在布拉格。布拉格是明媚的，布拉格是忧伤的，布拉格是神秘的，一千个人心中有一千个布拉格。布拉格汇聚了东欧纯粹的美，它不但拥有庞大的古建筑群，也在城市各处散落着先锋前卫的当代艺术：罗马式的地下室、哥特式的教堂、巴洛克式的

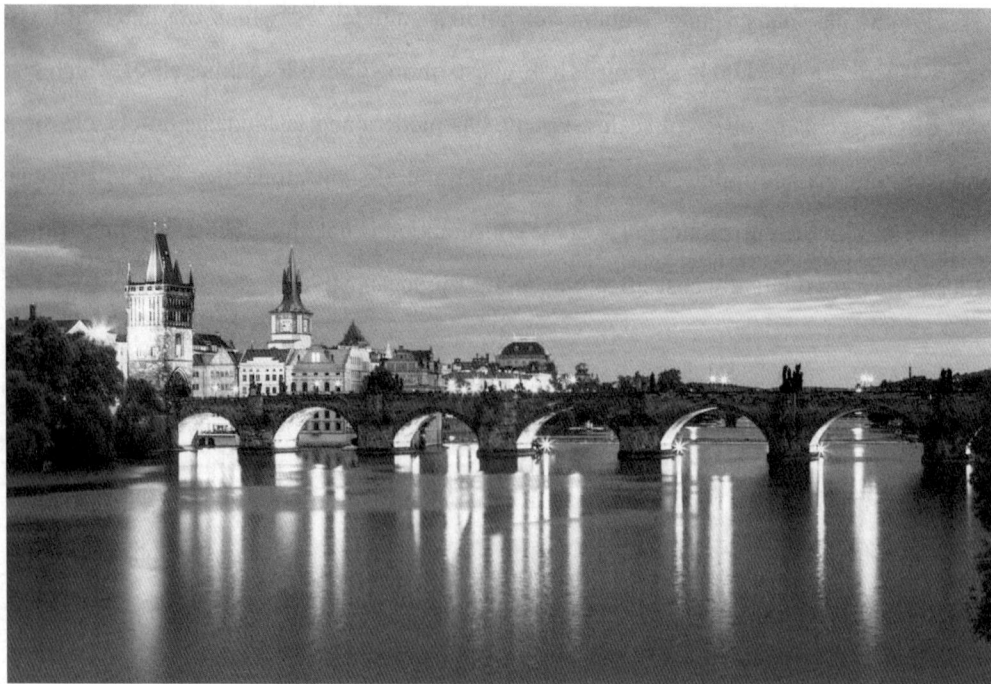

宫殿和花园、雕塑吊着的人、会跳舞的房子，处处能让人触摸到建筑及艺术的丰富多彩。

With a history of more than 900 years, Prague is the only city in the world that is listed as a World Cultural ·Heritage. In this ancient city, you feel like entering a fairy tale world: Prague Castle, St. Vitus Cathedral, Charlie Bridge, Old Town Square, Astronomical Clock, you will instinctively forget the time and get lost in Prague. Prague is bright, sad, and mysterious. There are a thousand Pragues in a thousand persons' eyes. Prague gathers the pure beauty of Eastern Europe. It not only has a huge group of ancient buildings, but also is scattered with avant-garde contemporary art all over the city, such as Romanesque basement, Gothic church, Baroque palace and garden, Hanging Sculpture, and Dancing House. People can touch the rich and colorful architecture and art everywhere.

◎查理大桥与弗兰兹·卡夫卡/Charlie Bridge and Franz Kafka

18座大桥横跨在伏尔塔瓦河之上，连接着布拉格两岸如梦如幻的红顶神话，其中查理大桥更是成为神话的焦点，拥有660年的历史。查理大桥是一座14世纪的大桥，是历代国王加冕游行的必经之路。查理大桥两侧护栏上有30尊圣者雕像，左右对称，每边15座，多为巴洛克风格，都出自17—18世纪著名捷克雕塑家之手，被欧洲人称为"欧洲的露天巴洛克塑像美术馆"。查理大桥承载着波西米亚辉煌的历史记忆和民族荣耀。卡夫卡曾说：他全部的灵感和生命都来源于伟大的查理大桥。卡夫卡是现代小说的奠基者和开拓者，更是一位思想敏锐的哲学洞见者，在布拉格黄金巷度过了他孤独压抑的一生。他的代表作《变形记》《城堡》《审判》直指现代人的变异和荒诞，艺术化地描写人性的悲观和孤独。你可以通过他的作品发现另一个看不见的布拉格。

Eighteen bridges across the Vltava River make the dream of red roof myths on both sides of Prague come true. Among them, Charlie Bridge has been the focus of the myth with a history of 660 years. Charley Bridge was built in the fourteenth century, which was the only way for the coronation processions of successive kings. There are 30 statues of saints on the guardrails on both sides of Charlie Bridge symmetrically. There are 15 statues on each side. Most of them are in Baroque style. They were created by famous Czech sculptors in the 17th—18th century. They are called "European Open-air Baroque Sculpture Gallery" in Europe. Charlie Bridge carries the glorious historical memory and national glory of Bohemia. Kafka once said: all his inspiration and life come from the great Charlie Bridge. Kafka is not only the founder and pioneer of modern novels, but also has a keen philosophical insight. He spent his lonely and depressed life in Prague's Golden Lane. His masterpieces like "The Metamorphosis", "Castle", and "The Trial" reveal the variation and absurdity of modern people and artistically describe the pessimism and loneliness of human nature. People can find another invisible Prague through his works.

◎音乐与咖啡 /Music and Coffee

作为欧洲排名第二的浪漫之都（第一是巴黎），布拉格的神秘与梦幻绕不过音乐与咖啡。布拉格最有名的节日就是布拉格之春国际音乐节，每年 5 月 12 日到 6 月 3 日，许多国际知名的乐团汇聚布拉格，歌剧院和市政厅聚集着乐队和热爱音乐的人们，查理大桥上也有音乐表演。除了音乐，散落在布拉格各个角落的各式咖啡馆也散发着浪漫神秘的色彩。百年咖啡馆 Cafe Louver 曾是爱因斯坦跟卡夫卡的最爱，以昆德拉为首的著名"布拉格之春"运动也在这里爆发；帝国咖啡馆环境奢华，被誉为世界十大最美咖啡馆；在城堡区你可以偶遇星巴克，俯瞰整个城市的美好。

As the second most romantic capital in Europe (Paris is the first), Prague's mystery and illusion cannot avoid music and coffee. Prague's most famous festival is the Prague Spring International Music Festival. From May 12 to June 3 every year, many well-known orchestras come to Prague. Bands and music lovers gather in Prague Opera House and City Hall. There are also music performances on Charlie Bridge. In addition to music, the various cafes scattered in every corner of Prague also give out romantic and mysterious atmosphere. Cafe Louver was once the favorite of Einstein and Kafka, and the famous

"Prague Spring" movement led by Kundera also broke out here; Cafe Imperial is known as the world's top 10 most beautiful cafes due to its luxurious environment; in the castle area, you can encounter Starbuck and overlook the beauty of the whole city.

3.9 葡萄牙里斯本概况
An Overview of Lisbon, Portugal

里斯本是葡萄牙共和国的首都，是欧洲大陆最西端的城市，距离大西洋不到 12 千米。里斯本港是国际海港。人口 286 万（2021 年），97% 以上居民信奉天主教。

Lisbon is the capital of the Republic of Portugal, the far western city on the European continent, less than 12 kilometers from the Atlantic Ocean. Lisbon Port is an international seaport. The population is 2.86 million (2021) and more than 97% of residents believe in Catholicism.

3.9.1 气候 /Climate

受大西洋暖流影响，里斯本气候良好，冬不结冰，夏不炎热。一二月份平均气温为 8℃，七八月份平均气温为 26℃。全年大部分时间风和日丽，温暖如春，舒适宜人。

Affected by the Atlantic warm current, Lisbon has a pleasant climate, neither freezing in winter nor too hot in summer. The average temperature in January and February is 8°C and that in July and August is 26°C. It is warm, sunny, comfortable and pleasant most of the year.

3.9.2 交通 /Transportation

里斯本机场距离市中心 7 千米，共有两座客运航站楼，即 1 号航站楼和 2 号航站楼，是西欧规模最大、设备最完善的机场之一。里斯本是全国的交通枢纽，是葡萄牙第一大港。里斯本市内交通以汽车和地铁为主，一共有 4 条地铁路线。

Lisbon Airport is 7 kilometers away from the city center. There are two passenger terminals, namely terminal 1 and terminal 2. It is one of the largest and most well-equipped airports in Western Europe. Lisbon is the transportation hub of the whole country and the largest port in Portugal. The traffic in Lisbon mainly depends on cars and subways, with a total of 4 subway lines.

3.9.3 展馆与酒店 /Exhibitions Venues and Hotels

里斯本国际展览中心总面积达 10 万平方米，分为 4 个展馆，每个展馆大概 1 万平方米，主要展览区域由这几个展馆组成，约 6 万平方米。被福布斯授予"全球最顶尖科技会议"称号的全球网络峰会每年就在里斯本国际展览中心举办，这里有 3 个会场，外加 1 个可容纳 1.5 万人的主舞台区。2019 年来自 163 个国家或地区的超过 7 万名参会者前来里斯本参加全球网络峰会，两年来给里斯本带来直接经济收入达 3 亿欧元。里斯本市内星级酒店数量从 2008 年的 105 家增长到 2017 年的 204 家，四星酒店平均价格达到 100 欧元左右。

Lisbon International Exhibition Center has a total area of 100,000 square meters and is divided into four exhibition halls, each of which is about 10,000 square meters. The main exhibition area is composed of these exhibition halls, about 60,000 square meters. Web Summit, awarded by Forbes as the "Top Technology Conference in the World", is held every year at the Lisbon International Exhibition Center, with three venues plus a main stage area that can accommodate 15,000 people. In 2019, more than 70,000 participants from 163 countries or regions came to Lisbon to attend Web Summit, bringing direct economic income of 300 million euros to Lisbon in the past two years. The number of star-rated hotels in Lisbon has increased from 105 in 2008 to 204 in 2017, with the average price of four-star hotels reaching about 100 euros.

3.9.4 会奖目的地优势 /Advantages of MICE Destination

葡萄牙旅游业的收入大约占 GDP 的 10%，里斯本已成为全球最佳旅游目的地之一。里斯本西部大西洋沿岸美丽的海滨浴场，每年吸引着来自世界各地 100 多万的游客。2017 年里斯本举办 ICCA 认证的国际会议 149 个，2018 年 152 个，2019 年 190 个，上升至全球第二位，仅次于巴黎。2019 年里斯本连续 3 年被 WTA 评为"世界最佳城市短期休闲目的地"，这不仅是里斯本的骄傲，也是葡萄牙的骄傲。

The income of Portugal's tourism industry accounts for about 10% of GDP. Lisbon has become one of the best tourist destinations in the world. The beautiful beach along the Atlantic coast in the west of Lisbon attracts more than 1 million tourists from all over the world every year. In 2017, Lisbon hosted 149 ICCA-certified international conferences, 152 in 2018, and 190 in 2019, rising to the second place in the world, second only to Paris. In 2019, Lisbon was rated "The World's Best Short-Term Leisure in City Destination" by WTA for three consecutive years, which was not only the pride of Lisbon, but also the pride of Portugal.

◎特色旅游资源 /Unique Tourism Resources

里斯本的老城区带着浓郁的沧桑感，欧洲最古老的 28 路有轨电车拥有近 150 年的历史，如今依然穿梭在狭窄的街道中。每个到葡萄牙旅游的客人，罗卡角是其必然的选择，这里是欧洲的"天涯海角"，是远航的水手们对陆地的最后记忆。罗卡角、非洲的好望角和南美的合恩角被誉为"世界三大名海角"，罗卡角的美艳难以用语言形容，一望无际的大西洋，在夕阳下闪耀着不同的光辉。

The old city of Lisbon has a strong sense of history. The oldest tram No.28 in Europe has a history of nearly 150 years, shuttling through narrow streets now. For every visitor to Portugal, Cape Roca is his /her inevitable choice. It is the "end of the earth" in Europe and the last memory of the sailors on the land. Cape Roca, Cape of Good Hope in Africa, and

Cape Horn in South America are known as "the Three Famous Cape of the World". The beauty of Cape Roca is hard to describe in words. The endless Atlantic Ocean shines with different brilliance in the sunset.

◎世界文化遗产 /World Cultural Heritage

1983 年贝伦塔与热罗尼莫斯修道院一起被列入世界遗产名录。贝伦塔建于 1500 年，已有 520 多年的历史，是里斯本的标志性建筑，见证了葡萄牙曾经辉煌的航海历史。葡萄牙航海家们在出海之前都会来到这里登上塔顶，再看一眼美丽的故乡，然后踏上遥远漫长的旅途。贝伦塔是大航海时代起航的起点，归航的终点。贝伦塔的塔身不高，但是外观装饰非常精美，融入了伊斯兰国家和东方的风格。热罗尼莫斯修道院被视为哥特式建筑的典范，是葡萄牙全盛时期修筑的艺术珍品，是为纪念葡萄牙人发现通往印度的海上航线所建。1755 年，里斯本突然发生罕见的 9 级大地震，整个里斯本毁于一旦，唯独这座修道院屹立不倒，拯救了在此祈祷的全体王室成员，因此更为其增添了神灵庇佑的神秘色彩。

Belem Tower was included in the world heritage list together with the Monastery of Jeronimos in 1983. The Belem Tower, built in 1500, has a history of more than 520 years. It is a landmark building in Lisbon. It has witnessed the glorious sailing history of Portugal. Before going out to sea, Portuguese navigators would climb to the top of the tower, have a look at the beautiful hometown, and then embark on a long and distant journey. Belem Tower is the starting point of sailing and the end of homing in the era of great navigation. Belem tower is not high, but the exterior decoration is very exquisite, which integrates Islamic countries and Oriental styles. As a model of Gothic architecture, the monastery of Jeronimus is an artistic treasure built in the heyday of Portugal. It was built to commemorate the discovery of the maritime route to India by the Portuguese. In 1755, a rare earthquake of magnitude 9 occurred in Lisbon, and the whole Lisbon was destroyed. Only this monastery stood up and saved all the members of the royal family praying here. Therefore, the mystery of divine protection was added.

◎欧洲物价最低城市之一/One of the Lowest Price Cities in Europe

作为欧洲面积最小、物价最低、最有趣的城市之一，里斯本超市的物价很多都在1欧元以内。面包不到1欧元，一打鸡蛋1欧元多一点，蔬菜水果新鲜且便宜。欧洲运输成本低，因为欧洲的高速公路发达，并且收费站少。欧洲的蔬菜水果是定期、定点生产分配的。全欧洲物流调配、大规模的生产及零售业的激烈竞争一起拉低了物价。

As one of the most interesting cities with the smallest area and the lowest price in Europe, the price of many supermarkets in Lisbon is less than 1 euro. Bread costs less than 1 euro, a dozen eggs may cost a little more than 1 euro, and vegetables and fruits are fresh and cheap. Europe's transportation cost is low, because the European highway is developed, and the toll station is few. Europe's vegetables and fruits are produced and distributed on a regular basis. Logistics deployment through Europe, large-scale production, and fierce competition in retail industry together bring down goods prices.

3.10 泰国曼谷概况
An Overview of Bangkok, Thailand

曼谷是泰国首都和最大的城市，别名"天使之城"，是繁华的国际一线城市，是贵金属和宝石的交易中心。曼谷旅游业十分发达，被评选为全球最受欢迎的旅游城市之一，每年有多达 200~300 场的国际会议在此举行。曼谷在 2019 年全球城市 500 强城市中排第 36 位。截至 2021 年 8 月，曼谷人口 800 万。

Bangkok is the capital and largest city of Thailand, also known as the "City of Angels". It is a prosperous international first-tier city and a trading center for precious metals and gems. Bangkok has a very developed tourism industry, and has been selected as one of the most popular tourist cities in the world. There are as many as 200—300 international conferences held here every year. Bangkok ranks 36th among the world's top 500 cities in 2019. By August 2021, the population of Bangkok is 8 million.

3.10.1 气候 /Climate

曼谷属热带季风气候，终年炎热，一年有明显的热季、雨季、凉季。每年 2 月至 4 月为热季，空气干燥，平均气温一般为 30℃左右，4 月平均气温高达 38℃。每年 5 月至 10 月是曼谷的雨季，全年 85% 的雨量集中在雨季。从 11 月到次年 1 月为凉季，平均气温在 25℃ ~27℃，凉季是旅游的最佳季节。

Bangkok has a tropical monsoon climate, which is hot all year round, with obvious hot season, rainy season, and cool season. The hot season is from February to April every year. The air is dry and the average temperature is generally about 30 ℃. Sometimes the highest average temperature can reach 38℃ in April. The rainy season in Bangkok is from May to October, 85% of the rainfall is concentrated in the rainy season. The cool season is from November to January of the next year, with an average temperature of 25℃ —27℃ . The cool season is the best season for tourism.

3.10.2 交通 /Transportation

曼谷有两个国际机场：廊曼国际机场，位于泰国曼谷北郊，又称为旧曼谷国际场。素万那普国际机场，位于泰国曼谷东郊，又称为新曼谷国际机场。曼谷市内的交通主要依赖轨道交通、公交、出租车等，目前轨道交通有 2 条轻轨、1 条地铁和 3 条机场快线。曼谷被称为全球最拥堵的城市。

There are two international airports in Bangkok: Don Mueang International Airport, located in the northern suburb of Bangkok, is also known as the Old Bangkok International Airport. Suvarnabhumi International Airport, located in the eastern suburb of Bangkok, is also known as the New Bangkok International Airport. The transportation in Bangkok mainly relies on rails, public transportation, and taxis. At present, there are two light rail transit (BTS), one subway (MRT), and three Airport Express lines. Bangkok is known as the most congested city in the world.

3.10.3 展馆与酒店 /Exhibitions Venues and Hotels

曼谷有 6,000 多处设施齐全的会议场地和 22 万平方米的展区面积。有 3 个主要展览中心：IMPACT 会展中心、曼谷国际贸易展览中心（BITEC）、诗丽吉皇后国家会议中心（QSNCC）。IMPACT 会展中心是亚洲规模最大、最现代化的会展场馆之一，拥有超过 14 万平方米可用的室内面积。曼谷国际贸易展览中心是泰国首屈一指的展览中心，拥有 19 个会场，可以根据实际需要调整具体面积。曼谷拥有众多本地品牌的四、五星级会议酒店及国际品牌的酒店，总共超过 7 万间客房，完全能满足团队前来举办会议和展览的需求。

Bangkok has more than 6,000 well-equipped conference venues and 220,000 square meters of exhibition area. There are three main exhibition centers: IMPACT Convention and Exhibition Center, Bangkok International Trade and Exhibition Center (BITEC), and Queen Sirikit National Convention Center (QSNCC). IMPACT Convention and Exhibition Center is one of the largest and most modern exhibition venues in Asia, with more than 140,000 square meters of usable indoor area. Bangkok International Trade and Exhibition Center is Thailand's leading exhibition center, which has 19 venues, and the specific area can be adjusted according to actual needs. Bangkok has many local brands of four-star and five-star conference hotels and international-brand hotels, with a total of more than 70,000 rooms, which can fully satisfy the team to hold conferences and exhibitions.

3.10.4　会奖目的地优势 /Advantages of MICE Destination

曼谷拥有众多的历史遗迹和各种佛寺，旅游配套完善，消费相对较低。种种因素使它成了全球每年游客访问量最多的城市，2018 年更是达到了惊人的 2,005 万人次。曼谷设有世界银行、世界卫生、国际劳工组织等 20 多个国际机构的区域办事处。2018 年曼谷举办 ICCA 认证的国际会议 135 个，位列全球第十，2019 年 124 个，位列全球第十三。

Bangkok has many historical sites and various Buddhist temples, complete tourism facilities, and relatively low consumption. Various factors make it host the largest number of tourists in the world every year. In 2018, it astonishingly reached 20.05 million. Bangkok has more than 20 regional offices of international institutions such as the World Bank, World Health Organization, and the International Labor Organization. In 2018, Bangkok held 135 ICCA-certified international conferences, ranking tenth in the world, and 124 in 2019, ranking thirteenth in the world.

◎特色旅游资源 /Unique Tourism Resources

曼谷是一个新潮、浪漫又文艺的国际大都市，随意逛逛各种寺庙、皇宫，吃吃热带水果，游游湄南河，寻找大街小巷中风格迥异的咖啡厅，从工业风、北欧风、田园风到性冷淡风应有尽有。曼谷一方面灯红酒绿、贫富悬殊，一方面又包容开放、知足向善。在慢悠悠的节奏中，每个人可以变得更快乐、更真实。

Bangkok is a fashionable, romantic, and artistic international metropolis. You can visit various temples and palaces, eat tropical fruits, tour the Mekong River, and look for coffee shops with different styles in the streets and alleys, ranging from industrial style, northern European style, rural style to sexual indifference. On the one hand, you can see feasting and revelry, huge gap between the rich and the poor in Bangkok; on the other hand, Bangkok is tolerant, open, content, and kind. Everyone here can become happier and more real in slow pace.

◎佛教之都 /Capital of Buddhism

曼谷佛教历史悠久，东方色彩浓厚，佛寺庙宇林立，建筑精致美观。曼谷是世界上佛寺最多的地方，有大小400多个佛教寺院。玉佛寺、卧佛寺、金佛寺被称为泰国三大国宝。泰国95%的民众信奉佛教，拥有32个成员的"世界佛教徒联谊会"总部设在曼谷。

Bangkok has a long history of Buddhism and strong oriental color. There are numerous Buddhist temples and exquisite buildings in Bangkok. Bangkok has the largest number of Buddhist temples in the world, with more than 400 Buddhist temples in size. Wat Phra Kaew, Wat Pho, and Wat Traimit are known as the three national treasures of Thailand. In Thailand, 95% of the people believe in Buddhism. The World Fellowship of Buddhists, which has 32 members, is headquartered in Bangkok.

◎曼谷不夜城 /Bangkok Never Sleeps

泰国的消费水平很低，曼谷更是一座不夜城。泰式按摩及酒吧令人流连忘返。泰式按摩是跪式服务，以活动关节为主，不同于中式按摩，它能使人快速消除疲劳，恢复体能，有保健预防、健体美容的功效。泰式按摩是古代泰王招待皇家贵宾的最高礼节。2019年泰式按摩被列入世界非物质文化遗产名单。当地的酒吧也非常具有特色，只要走到曼谷的酒吧街就能够感受到不同，在这里可以看到精彩非凡的"人妖"表演。

Thailand's consumption level is very low, and Bangkok is a city that never sleeps. "Thai massage" and bars make you forget to go back. Thai massage is a kneeling service, which mainly focuses on moving joints, different from Chinese massage. It can quickly eliminate fatigue, restore physical fitness, and has the effects of health care, disease prevention and beauty. Thai massage is the highest etiquette for the king of Thailand to entertain Royal guests in ancient times. In 2019, Thai massage was listed in World Intangible Cultural Heritage. The local bar is also very distinctive. If you walk to the bar street of Bangkok, you can feel the difference and see wonderful "katoey" performances here.

3.11 澳大利亚悉尼概况
An Overview of Sydney, Australia

澳大利亚悉尼

悉尼，新南威尔士州的首府，位于南半球的澳大利亚东南沿岸，是澳大利亚面积最大、人口最多的城市。悉尼市区人口约 463 万（2020 年），大悉尼都会区由悉尼市区和 33 个郊区组成。悉尼是世界著名的旅游城市及国际大都市。

Sydney, the capital of New South Wales, is located on the southeastern coast of Australia in Southern Hemisphere. It is the largest and most populous city in Australia. The urban population of Sydney is about 4.63 million (2020). The greater Sydney metropolitan area is composed of Sydney urban area and 33 suburbs. Sydney is a world-famous tourism city and international metropolis.

3.11.1 气候 /Climate

悉尼属于副热带湿润气候，全年降雨，夏天和冬天的雨量相当平均。最暖的月份是 1 月，沿海地区的气温是 18.6℃ ~25.8℃，历史记录陆地的最高温度为 45.3℃。最冷的月份是七月，平均极端值是 8.0℃ ~16.2℃，陆地的最低值是 2.1℃。

Sydney has a humid subtropical climate, with rain throughout the year. The rainfall in summer and winter is fairly even. The warmest month is January, the temperature in coastal areas is 18.6°C—25.8°C, and the highest temperature recorded on land is 45.3℃ .

The coldest month is July, the average extreme temperature is 8.0°C—16.2°C, the minimum temperature on land is 2.1°C.

3.11.2 交通 /Transportation

悉尼金斯福德·史密斯国际机场是全澳大利亚最繁忙的机场，也是全球持续运营时间最长的机场之一。地铁连接 T1 国际候机楼、T2 国内候机楼和 T3 澳航航站楼。悉尼拥有发达的铁路运输系统。悉尼的铁路网全部集中在大悉尼都会区的市环线以内。悉尼配备完善的高速公路系统，但主要都在城郊。太平洋高速公路是悉尼的主要公路。

Sydney Kingsford Smith International Airport is the busiest airport in Australia and one of the longest operating airports in the world. The metro connects T1 international terminal, T2 domestic terminal, and T3 Qantas terminal. Sydney has a well-developed railway transportation system. Sydney's rail network is all concentrated within the metropolitan area of greater Sydney. Sydney is equipped with a complete highway system, but mainly in the suburbs. The Pacific Expressway is the main highway in Sydney.

3.11.3 展馆与酒店 /Exhibitions Venues and Hotels

悉尼拥有澳大利亚首屈一指的综合性会议、展览中心。悉尼国际会议中心坐落于达令港的中心区域，场馆不仅拥有约 35,000 平方米的展览空间，还有一个能够饱览达令港风光的约 5,000 平方米的露天活动平台，集会议、展览和娱乐于一体。2018 年，悉尼国际会议中心成功举办了逾 700 场核心会议及活动，这一傲人成绩向世界展示了悉尼国际会议中心出类拔萃的会奖服务。悉尼的许多酒店地理位置优越，紧邻海滩。至 2025 年，悉尼市场将新增 11,600 个客房。悉尼的酒店全年入住率为 87%，是世界上酒店入住率最高的城市之一。

Sydney has Australia's leading comprehensive conference and exhibition center. Sydney International Convention Center is located in the central area of Darling Harbor. The venue not only has about 35,000 square meters of exhibition space, but also has a about 5,000 square meters open-air activity platform which can enjoy the scenery of

Darling Harbor, integrating conference, exhibition, and entertainment. In 2018, Sydney International Convention Center successfully held more than 700 core conferences and activities, which demonstrated the outstanding MICE service of Sydney International Convention Center to the world. Many hotels in Sydney are ideally located close to the beach. By 2025, there will be 11,600 new rooms in the Sydney market. The occupancy rate of hotels in Sydney is 87%, which is one of the highest in the world.

3.11.4　会奖目的地优势 /Advantages of MICE Destination

悉尼在 2018 年世界城市排名中排第七，2019 年位列第六名，2020 年入选"2020 全球避暑名城榜"。 2019 年悉尼共举办 ICCA 认证的国际会议 93 个。在亚太地区顶尖会议及活动城市评选中，悉尼再次登顶。

Sydney ranked seventh in the 2018 World City Rankings, and sixth in 2019. In 2020, it was selected as the "2020 Global Summer Cities List". In 2019, Sydney held a total of 93 ICCA-certified international conferences. In the selection of the top conference and

event cities in the Asia-Pacific region, Sydney once again reached the top.

◎特色旅游资源 /Unique Tourism Resources

悉尼是澳大利亚古老而迷人的城市。悉尼既有迷人的自然风光，又有独特的历史文化，还有特有物种。达令港、邦迪海滩、歌剧院和港湾大桥闻名遐迩。悉尼歌剧院是悉尼代表性的建筑物，也是澳大利亚的象征。2007 年悉尼歌剧院被联合国教科文组织评为世界文化遗产。邦迪海滩沙质柔软、风景优美，是欣赏日出、日落的最佳胜地，还是日光浴和冲浪的绝佳地点。同时，为世人熟知的动物包括袋鼠、考拉、澳洲野狗、鸭嘴兽、毛鼻袋熊等都是澳洲特有物种。悉尼因其丰富的生物多样性和特有物种吸引了大量的游客及研究者。

Sydney is an ancient and fascinating city in Australia. Sydney has fascinating natural scenery, unique history and culture, and rare species. Darling Harbor, Bondi Beach, Opera House, and Harbor Bridge are famous all over the world. Opera House is a representative building of Sydney and a symbol of Australia. In 2007, Opera House was listed in World Cultural Heritage by UNESCO. With soft sand and beautiful scenery, Bondi Beach is not only the best place to enjoy the sunrise and sunset, but also a great place for sunbathing and surfing. Meanwhile, most well-known animals including kangaroos, koalas, Australian wild dogs, platypuses, and wombats are all endemic to Australia. Sydney is attracting many tourists and researchers due to its rich biodiversity and endemic species.

◎世界最宜居城市 /The Most Livable City in the World

悉尼拥有高度发达的金融业、制造业和旅游业。许多顶级跨国企业、国内外金融机构的总部均扎根悉尼。美丽的海滩、茂密的森林、充足的阳光、自由的空间让悉尼被联合国评为全球最适宜人类居住的城市之一，连续多年占据全球宜居城市排名前十位，2019 全球最宜居城市排名升至第三。

Sydney has a highly developed financial industry, manufacturing industry, and tourism industry. Many top multinational enterprises, domestic, and foreign financial institutions are based in Sydney. With beautiful beaches, dense forests, plenty of sunshine, and free space, Sydney has been rated as one of the most livable cities in the world by the United Nations, occupying the top 10 livable cities in the world for many consecutive years, and rising to the third in 2019.

◎体育赛事举办地 /Venue of Sports Events

悉尼是一座崇尚运动的城市，拥有世界一流的体育场馆。奥林匹克公园和悉尼足球体育馆为大型体育赛事提供了场地。澳大利亚体育场是全国橄榄球联赛（NRL）的总决赛场地。悉尼是澳大利亚橄榄球联盟的总部，16 支全国橄榄球联赛球队中的 8 支在悉尼。悉尼的海港和沙滩适合举办各种各样的水上运动。悉尼是多项重要国际体育赛事的举办城市，1938 年英联邦运动会、2000 年奥运会及 2003 年橄榄球世界杯赛均在悉尼举办。

Sydney is a city that advocates sports. The Olympic Park and Sydney Football Stadium provide venues for large-scale sports events. The Australian stadium is the venue for the finals of the National Football League (NRL). Sydney is the headquarter of the Australian Rugby League. Eight of the 16 NRL teams are based in Sydney. Sydney's seaports and beaches are suitable for all kinds of water sports. Sydney is the host city of many important international sports events, such as 1938 Commonwealth Games, 2000 Olympic Games, and 2003 Rugby World Cup.

3.l2 韩国首尔概况
An Overview of Seoul, Republic of Korea

韩国首尔

　　首尔，大韩民国首都，是韩国政治、经济、科技、教育、文化中心。首尔是世界第十大城市，全市下辖 25 个区。首尔首都圈人口几乎占韩国总人口的一半，人口密度极高，是世界十大金融中心之一，消费者物价指数居世界第五。2018 年 11 月，世界城市排名发布，首尔进入世界一线城市行列。

Seoul, the capital of the Republic of Korea, is the political, economic, technological, educational, and cultural center of Republic of Korea. Seoul is the tenth largest city in the world, with 25 districts under its jurisdiction. Seoul metropolitan area accounts for nearly half of the total population of Republic of Korea. With extremely high population density, it is one of the top ten financial centers in the world, and its consumer price index ranks fifth in the world. In November 2018, the world city rankings were released, and Seoul entered the ranks of the world's first tier cities.

3.12.1　气候 /Climate

　　首尔是温带季风气候，四季分明。春、秋季雨水少，气候温暖，适宜旅游。6 月至 9 月中旬为夏季，月平均温度为 20℃～ 27℃，12 月至 2 月为冬季，比同纬度的其他城市气温略低，月平均温度为 –5℃～ 0℃。

Seoul has a temperate monsoon climate with four distinct seasons. It rains less in Spring and Autumn when climate is warm and suitable for tourism. Summer lasts from

June to Mid September and the monthly average temperature is 20℃—27℃. From December to February is winter whose temperature is lower than that in other cities at the same latitude, and the monthly average temperature is -5℃—0℃ .

3.12.2　交通 /Transportation

首尔主要有两个机场：仁川国际机场（ICN）是韩国的民用机场。金浦国际机场（GMP）是首尔第二大国际机场，专门运营国内航线，还有到中国上海、北京的专线。首尔同釜山、仁川等主要城市有高速公路相通。首尔地铁是世界前五大载客量的铁路系统，载客量位居全球第三位。

There are mainly two airports in Seoul. Incheon International Airport (ICN) is a civil airport in Republic of Korea. Jinpu International Airport (GMP) is Seoul's second largest international airport, specialized in domestic flight lines, as well as special lines to Shanghai and Beijing, China. Seoul is connected with Busan, Incheon, and other major cities by express ways. Seoul Metro is one of the world's top five railway systems with the third largest passenger capacity in the world.

3.12.3　展馆与酒店 /Exhibitions Venues and Hotels

COEX 首尔国际会议中心是韩国顶级的会议中心，同时也是韩国最大的展览展馆，2010 年的 G20 峰会和 2012 年的核安全峰会都在此举办，每年 365 天该展馆举办的展会络绎不绝。首尔拥有 256 家酒店，共 43,000 间客房，从五星级到经济型的住宿应有尽有，美食精致，环境安全。

COEX Seoul International Convention Center is the top conference center in Republic of Korea and the largest exhibition hall in Republic of Korea. Both the G20 Summit in 2010 and the Nuclear Security Summit in 2012 were held here, with an endless stream of exhibitions held 365 days a year. Seoul has 256 Hotels with 43,000 rooms, ranging from five-star to economical accommodation, providing exquisite food and safe environment.

3.12.4　会奖目的地优势 /Advantages of MICE Destination

首尔市一直致力于会奖旅游业的集中培育。首尔曾获"2015 年世界首届一指的会奖旅游城市""最高国际商务会议目的地""最佳会奖旅游城市"等称号，2017—2019 年首尔共举办 ICCA 认证的国际会议 378 个。首尔是极具魅力的会奖目的地城市。

Seoul has focused on the development of MICE industry in recent years. Seoul has won the "2015 World's Top Award Tourism City" "The Best International Business Meetings Destination", and "The Best MICE City". During 2017—2019, Seoul hosted 378 ICCA certified international conferences. Seoul is a very attractive MICE destination city.

◎特色旅游资源 /Unique Tourism Resources

首尔是韩国历史与文化的中心，既有景福宫等朝鲜时代的古代宫殿，又有最尖端的综合文化设施。首尔拥有多变动态的城市景观、精彩纷呈的娱乐选择、丰富精致的美食、多姿多彩的节庆：每年四月的樱花节、五月的燃灯节、十月初的鼓乐节等节庆充满活力，弘扬了韩国的传统文化。首尔既是现代化大都市，又不失古典韵味。

Seoul is the center of history and culture of Republic of Korea. There are not only ancient palaces in the Korean era such as Gyeongbokgung Palace, but also the most sophisticated comprehensive cultural facilities. Seoul has a dynamic urban landscape, wonderful entertainment choices, rich and exquisite food, and colorful festivals: the Cherry Blossom Festival in April, the Lantern Festival in May, and the Drum Festival in early October are full of vitality and carry forward the traditional culture of Republic of Korea. Seoul is a modern metropolis with classical charm.

◎亚洲时尚之都 /Fashion Capital of Asia

韩剧在亚洲各国具有较大的影响力，韩国文化的符号与元素通过韩剧走进电视受众的心中。首尔借助偶像或偶像团体充分发挥"韩流"文化的影响力，带动本国时尚的发展。与世界四大时装周相比，首尔时装周品牌更贴近亚洲人，

自由奔放、流行元素和艺术文化都幻化在细节上。东京及首尔的时装设计代表了亚洲时装的顶尖水平。

Asian countries are greatly influenced by Korean dramas, through which symbols and elements of Korean culture enter the hearts of TV audience. With the help of idols or idol groups, Seoul gives full play to the influence of "Korean Wave" culture and promotes the development of its own fashion. Compared with the four major fashion weeks in the world, Seoul Fashion Week brands are much closer to Asians. Free and unrestrained, popular elements, and artistic culture are illusory in terms of details. The fashion design in Tokyo and Seoul represents the top level of Asian fashion.

◎数字化程度极高 /High Degree of Digitization

首尔数字化程度很高，网速和数字机会指数均居世界首位。韩国因特网起步早，20 世纪末政府提供财政补贴和政策支持实现"光纤到户"。韩国三大电信运营商的竞争在充分的监管机制中变成良性竞争，并从中获益。韩国政府 2020 年 6 月份宣布，计划至 2025 年，将建设大数据平台、第五代移动通信（5G）、人工智能等数字产业基础设施，以数字化、绿色化和稳就业为方向投入约 76 万亿韩元。

Seoul is highly digitized, with Internet speed and digital opportunity index ranking first in the world. The Internet in Republic of Korea started early. At the end of the 20th century, the government provided financial subsidies and policy support to achieve "fiber to the home". Under adequate regulatory mechanism, the competition among the three telecom operators in Republic of Korea kept healthy and benefited from it. The Republic of Korea government announced in June 2020 that it plans to build big data platforms, fifth-generation mobile communications (5G), artificial intelligence, and other digital industry infrastructure by 2025, and invest about 76 trillion won in the direction of digitization, greening, and job stabilization.

俄罗斯莫斯科

3.13 俄罗斯莫斯科概况
An Overview of Moscow, Russia

莫斯科是俄罗斯联邦首都。它是俄罗斯政治、经济、文化和金融中心，也是欧亚大陆极其重要的交通枢纽，迄今已有 800 多年的历史，是国际化大都市，也是世界著名的古城。

Moscow is the capital of the Russian Federation. It is the political, economic, cultural and financial center of Russia, and an extremely important transportation hub in Eurasia. It has a history of more than 800 years. It is an international metropolis and a world-famous ancient city.

3.13.1 气候 /Climate

莫斯科属于温和的温带大陆性湿润气候，极端天气十分频繁。冬季长，降雪量大，冰雪消融期长，平均年积雪期长达 146 天。夏天可能气温陡降，阴雨连绵。

Moscow has a mild and humid temperate continental climate with frequent extreme weather. Moscow has long winter with long ice and snow melting period. The annual average snowfall is 146 days. In summer, the temperature may drop sharply and it will rain continuously.

3.13.2　交通 /Transportation

莫斯科拥有 4 座机场，与大部分欧洲国家首都和纽约、东京等外国城市有直达航线。莫斯科交通发达，是俄罗斯全国铁路、公路、河运和航空的枢纽。市内交通以地铁和公共汽车为主要工具。莫斯科的地铁历史悠久，拥有 13 条线路以及 200 多个车站，被公认为是全世界最美的地下艺术殿堂。

Moscow has four airports with direct routes to most European capitals and foreign cities such as New York and Tokyo. Moscow owns developed transportation systems and is the hub of railway, highway, river transportation, and aviation. Metros and buses are the main means of city transportation. Moscow's metro has a long history, with 13 lines and more than 200 stations. It is recognized as the most beautiful underground art palace in the world.

3.13.3　展馆与酒店 /Exhibitions Venues and Hotels

俄罗斯五大展览中心中有 3 个位于莫斯科：莫斯科国际展览中心是俄罗斯最大的国际展览场所，场馆总面积超过 250,000 平方米，展览总面积 150,000 平方米。全俄展览中心是俄罗斯最早的展览中心，内有 250 多个雄伟秀丽的各式建筑，还有宜人的公园、别致的喷泉及池塘。第三个展览中心就是现代化的克罗库斯国际展览中心。在莫斯科，有不少名流政要下榻的老牌豪华酒店，也不乏适合家庭旅行的经济型酒店，靠近地铁站，出游十分便利。

Of Russia's five major exhibition centers, three are in Moscow: Moscow International Exhibition Center is the largest international exhibition in Russia. The total space of the venue is over 250,000 square meters, and the total exhibition space is 150,000 square meters. All-Russia Exhibition Center is the earliest exhibition center in Russia. There are more than 250 magnificent and beautiful buildings, as well as pleasant parks, unique fountains and ponds. The third one is modern Crocus Expo International Exhibition Center. In Moscow, there are many old luxury hotels where celebrities and politicians stay, and there are also many budget hotels close to the subways which are convenient and suitable for families.

3.13.4　会奖目的地优势 /Advantages of MICE Destination

2019 年 11 月莫斯科首次击败伦敦、巴黎和圣彼得堡，赢得了号称"旅游界奥斯卡"的旅游业国际权威大奖 WTA 的最重要奖项——最佳旅游目的地城市奖。这一枚优质奖章是莫斯科巩固其国际旅游中心地位的标志。

For the first time in November 2019, Moscow defeated London, Paris, and St. Petersburg and won the "Best Tourism Destination City" award, the most important one of "World Travel Awards", which is known as the "Oscar in tourism industry". This high-quality medal is a symbol of Moscow's consolidation of its position as an international tourism center.

◎特色旅游资源 /Unique Tourism Resources

莫斯科城市规划优美，掩映在一片绿海之中，故有"森林中的首都"之美誉。莫斯科拥有众多名胜古迹，克里姆林宫、新圣女修道院、金色环城路、寂

静的阿尔巴特街都令人印象深刻。与新圣女修道院毗邻的新圣女公墓将多彩的历史人物、精湛的艺术雕塑、灵秀的园林胜景，完美和谐地融为一体。这里埋葬着俄罗斯民族历代的精英和骄傲，是俄罗斯著名知识分子和各界名流的长眠之地。无论是天才，还是绝代佳人，终将化为尘土。惟有智者的精神财富、独立思想才能永存于世。

Moscow has a beautiful urban planning, which is reflected in a green sea, so it boosts the reputation of "Capital in the Forest". Moscow has many places of interest. The Kremlin, Ensemble of the Novodevichy Convent, the Golden Ring Road, and the silent Arbat Street are all impressive. Novodevichy Cemetery adjacent to Ensemble of the Novodevichy Convent perfectly integrates historical figures, exquisite art sculptures and beautiful garden scenery. The elite and pride of the Russian nation of all ages are buried here who are Russia's famous intellectuals and celebrities from all walks of life. Whether a genius or a beautiful woman, he or she will eventually turn to dust. Only the spiritual wealth and independent thought of the wise can survive forever.

◎ 克里姆林宫与红场 /The Kremlin and Red Square

作为政权的至高点，克里姆林宫吸引着全世界的目光。在这里伊凡雷帝开始了他恐怖的统治；拿破仑注视着莫斯科的燃烧；列宁实施了无产阶级专政；斯大林清理了阶级队伍；赫鲁晓夫抗击了冷战；戈尔巴乔夫开创了体制改革；叶利钦开启了新俄罗斯的篇章；普京引领俄罗斯走向复兴。克里姆林宫这一世界闻名的建筑群，像是一部巨大的词典，详尽地记录了俄罗斯的历史。解开新旧俄罗斯之谜要从了解克里姆林宫开始。红场是莫斯科最古老的广场，见证了许多重大历史事件，是国家举行各种大型庆典及阅兵活动的中心地点，是世界著名旅游景点。1990 年，克里姆林宫与红场被列入世界文化遗产名录。

As the summit of political power, the Kremlin attracts the attention of the whole world. Here Ivan the Terrible began his reign of terror; Napoleon watched the burning of Moscow; Lenin carried out the dictatorship of the proletariat; Stalin cleaned up the class ranks; Khrushchev fought the Cold War; Gorbachev initiated the reform of the system; Yeltsin opened the chapter of new Russia; Putin led Russia to rejuvenation. The Kremlin, a world-famous building complex, is like a huge dictionary, which records the history of Russia in detail. To seek the mystery of old and new Russia, we should start from understanding the Kremlin. Red Square is the oldest square in Moscow, witnessing many important historical events. It is the central place for holding various large-scale celebrations and military parades. It is a world-famous tourist attraction. In 1990, the Kremlin and Red Square were listed in the World Cultural Heritage List.

◎文学和音乐的殿堂 /Palace of literature and Music

莫斯科是一座充满历史故事以及文学和音乐气息的城市。文学大师托尔斯泰、普希金、契诃夫、高尔基，音乐大师柴科夫斯基、肖斯塔科维奇、格林卡，文学名著《战争与和平》《静静的顿河》《罪与罚》及歌曲《莫斯科郊外的晚上》《喀秋莎》《小路》充满着时代的气息，影响了一代又一代的年轻人。莫斯科国立柴可夫斯基音乐学院是全世界最大和最著名的高等音乐学府之一，每年一度的柴可夫斯基钢琴比赛是产生杰出钢琴演奏家的摇篮。

Moscow is a city full of historical stories, literature and music. Literary masters like Tolstoy, Pushkin, Chekov, and Gorky, music masters like Tchaikovsky, Shostakovich, Glinka have produced a lot of masterpieces, such as *War and Peace*, *Quiet Flows Don*, *Crime and Punishment*, and the song *Moscow Nights*, *Katyusha*, *The Path*. Their masterpieces are full of the atmosphere of the times and have influenced the young people of generations. The Moscow State Tchaikovsky Conservatory is one of the largest and most famous institutions of music in the world. The annual Tchaikovsky Piano Competition is the cradle of outstanding pianists.

3.14 意大利米兰概况
An Overview of Milan, Italy

意大利米兰

米兰位于意大利北部，意大利第二大城市，是世界八大都会区之一。米兰分为3级：米兰大都会区、米兰省、米兰市。米兰都会区包含8个省和272个城市，米兰大都会区人口755万。

Located in northern Italy, Milan is the second largest city in Italy, and one of the eight metropolitan areas in the world. Milan is of three levels: Milan Metropolitan Area, Milan Province, Milan City. The metropolitan area of Milan contains 8 provinces and 272 cities, with a population of 7.55 million.

3.14.1 气候 /Climate

米兰属于地中海气候：夏季炎热干燥，冬季温和多雨。冬雨夏干的气候特征，在世界各种气候类型中可谓独树一帜。

Milan has a Mediterranean climate: summers are hot and dry, and winters are mild and rainy. The climatic characteristics of rainy winter and dry summer are unique among the various climate types in the world.

3.14.2 交通 /Transportation

米兰一共有4个机场，其中3个为大型国际机场，其中马尔彭萨国际机场（MXP）是欧洲最主要的大机场之一，另外两个国际机场为利纳特国际机场（LIN）

和贝尔加莫国际机场（BGY）。米兰拥有 100 多个火车站，其中米兰中央火车站是欧洲规模最大的火车站。

There are four airports in Milan, three of which are large international airports. Among them, Malpensa International Airport (MXP) is one of the most important major airports in Europe. The other two international airports are Linate International Airport (LIN) and Bergamo International Airport (BGY). Milan has more than 100 railway stations, of which Milan Central Station is the largest railway station in Europe.

3.14.3　展馆与酒店 /Exhibitions Venues and Hotels

米兰国际展览中心是世界上最大的展览中心，也是世界上设备最先进的展览场地。米兰国际展览中心包括米兰展览馆、米兰 RHO 展览馆、米兰城市展览馆和米兰展览中心。总占地面积近 430 万平方米，展览面积近 140 万平方米，米兰国际展览中心是世界展览业巨头，在国际上有着举足轻重的地位。

Milan International Exhibition Center is the world's largest exhibition center and the world's most advanced exhibition venue. Milan International Exhibition Center includes Milan Exhibition Hall, Milan RHO Exhibition Hall, Milan City Exhibition Hall, and Milan Exhibition Center. With a total area of nearly 4.3 million square meters and an exhibition area of nearly 1.4 million square meters, the Milan International Exhibition Center is a world exhibition industry giant and has a pivotal position in the world.

3.14.4　会奖目的地优势 /Advantages of MICE Destination

米兰是欧洲四大经济中心（巴黎、伦敦、柏林、米兰）之一，世界顶级的国际大都市，也是世界时尚与设计之都及世界展览之城。著名的米兰国际家具展、米兰三年展、米兰时装周、米兰设计周、米兰建筑设计展等都大力推动米兰成为世界会奖目的地。

Milan is one of the four major economic centers in Europe (Paris, London, Berlin, and Italy). It is the world's top international metropolis, the world's fashion and design capital, and the world's exhibition city. The famous Milan International Furniture Fair, Milan Triennale, Milan Fashion Week, Milan Design Week, Milan Architectural Design Exhibition, etc. have vigorously promoted Milan as a global MICE destination.

◎特色旅游资源 /Unique Tourism Resources

米兰孕育了许多欧洲顶级品牌，如普拉达、范思哲等，引领时尚理念的变革，对时尚潮流有着非常敏锐的嗅觉。米兰时装周与巴黎时装周、纽约时装周、伦敦时装周并称四大时装周，其出现最晚却早已冠称其他三者之上，被认为是世界时装设计和消费的风向标。

Milan has bred many top European brands, such as Prada, Versace, leading the transformation of fashion concepts, having a very keen sense of fashion trends. Milan Fashion Week, Paris Fashion Week, New York Fashion Week, and London Fashion Week are called the four major fashion weeks. Milan Fashion week appeared at the latest but have already been named above the other three. It is considered to be the vane of world fashion design and consumption.

◎歌剧与艺术之都 /Capital of Opera and Arts

意大利歌剧闻名世界，米兰更是歌剧的中心。世界最为著名的斯卡拉歌剧院代表着世界歌剧艺术的最高峰，有歌剧麦加之称。米兰更是艺术之都，拥有众多的美术馆和博物馆。达芬奇的《最后的晚餐》和众多手稿，米开朗基罗生前最后一个雕塑，拉斐尔、毕加索等大师的绘画收藏在米兰的各个博物馆中。

Italian opera is famous all over the world. Milan is the center of opera. The world's most famous La Scala represents the highest peak of the world's opera art, and is known as the opera Mecca. Milan is also a capital of art. Milan has many art galleries and museums. Da Vinci's *Last Supper* and many manuscripts, the last sculpture of Michelangelo during his lifetime, and the paintings of Rafael, Picasso, and other masters are collected in Milan's various museums.

◎享有多重头衔/Multiple Titles

米兰是世界足球之城，AC 米兰队和国际米兰队闻名于世。著名的圣西罗 /
梅阿查球场是世界各地球迷心目中的圣地，1990 年世界杯的开幕式也在此举办。
米兰又是世界天主教的重镇，地位仅次于罗马教廷。米兰拥有世界第二大教堂、
世界第一大哥特式教堂：米兰大教堂。

Milan is a world football city. AC Milan and Inter Milan are well-known in the world.
The famous San Siro/Meazza Stadium is a holy place for fans around the world. The
opening ceremony of the 1990 World Cup was also held here. Milan is also an important
city of Catholicism with high influence in the world, ranking second only to the Roman
Curia. Milan has the second largest cathedral in the world and the world's largest Gothic
church: Church of Duomo.

3.15 美国拉斯维加斯概况
An Overview of Las Vegas, USA

拉斯维加斯于 1905 年建市，是美国内华达州最大的城市，享有极高的国际声誉，位列 2019 年全球城市 500 强榜单第 77 位。拉斯维加斯市区人口 64 万（2018 年），大都会人口 222 万。

Established in 1905, Las Vegas is the largest city in Nevada, USA, and enjoys a high international reputation. It is ranked 77th in the 2019 Global 500 City List. Downtown Las Vegas population is 640,000 (2018), and the metropolitan area population is 2.22 million.

3.15.1 气候/Climate

因位于内华达州的沙漠边缘、边境，拉斯维加斯全年高温，气候四季分明。夏季是典型的沙漠性气候，正午的温度常常高达 38℃，晚间的温度相对凉爽。冬季整体上是气候温和适宜，白天的平均温度在 15℃左右，周围都是沙漠，和死亡谷一样干燥。

Located on the edge and border of the desert in Nevada, Las Vegas is hot all year round, and the weather is distinct in four seasons. Summer has a typical desert climate. The temperature at noon is often as high as 38℃, and the temperature at night is relatively cool. In winter, the climate is generally mild and suitable, and the average daytime temperature is around 15℃. Surrounded by desert, Las Vegas is as dry as Death Valley.

3.15.2 交通 /Transportation

位于拉斯维加斯市中心以南约 8 千米的帕拉代斯的拉斯维加斯麦卡伦国际机场拥有 3 座客运航站楼，即 T1、T2 和 T3 航站楼，是世界上客流量较大的机场之一。

Las Vegas McCarran International Airport, located in Parades, about 8 kilometers south of Las Vegas city center, has three passenger terminals, namely T1, T2, and T3, which is one of the airports with world's highest passenger flow.

3.15.3 展馆与酒店 /Exhibitions Venues and Hotels

拉斯维加斯会展中心和拉斯维加斯金沙会议展览中心是拉斯维加斯两大展览会议中心。拉斯维加斯会展中心展馆面积 30 万平方米，是世界上最大的单层会议中心，也是目前世界上最繁忙、最先进的多功能场馆之一，位于拉斯维加斯山谷的中心地带。拉斯维加斯金沙会展中心展览面积超过 20 万平方米，可容纳人员 10 万人以上。拉斯维加斯位于荒漠之中，却拥有世界一流水平的酒店，许多酒店内景非常有特色，酒店住宿税率 9%，远远低于芝加哥和纽约。

Las Vegas Convention and Exhibition Center and Las Vegas Sands Convention and Exhibition Center are two major convention and exhibition centers in Las Vegas. With an area of 300,000 square meters, Las Vegas Convention and Exhibition Center is the world's largest single-story convention center and one of the busiest and most advanced multi-functional venues in the world. It is located in the center of Las Vegas Valley. Las Vegas Sands Convention and Exhibition Center has an exhibition area of more than 200,000 square meters and can accommodate more than 100,000 people. Las Vegas is located in the desert, but it has world-class hotels. Many of the hotel interior features are unique and the hotel accommodation tax rate is 9%, which is far lower than Chicago and New York.

3.15.4 会奖目的地优势 /Advantages of MICE Destination

拉斯维加斯世贸中心再次被 WTA 评为 2017 年度全球最佳会议场所，这是拉斯维加斯世贸中心连续 5 年获此殊荣。2016 年，拉斯维加斯会议中心曾创下

4,290 万游客的接待记录，而其中高达 630 万人是商旅参会人士。

Las Vegas World Trade Center was once again named the World's Best Conference Venue in 2017 by WTA. This was the fifth consecutive year that Las Vegas World Trade Center had won this award. In 2016, the Las Vegas Convention Center set a record of 42.9 million visitors, of which up to 6.3 million were business travelers.

◎特色旅游资源 /Unique Tourism Resources

拉斯维加斯作为一座以赌博业为中心的世界知名度假城市，是一个不折不扣的不夜赌城。它的气质犹如一枚硬币的两面，一面是地狱，另一面是天堂。独一无二的博彩业让它每年的游客数达到 3,900 万。同时，拉斯维加斯拥有多元的文化娱乐产业，除了繁华的街景、各种美食、放肆的购物体验之外，拉斯维加斯还有独特的城市玩法——表演秀！O 秀、魔术秀、梦中水秀等让各行各业各个年龄阶段的人都能成为他们的粉丝。

Las Vegas, as a world-renowned resort city centered on the gambling industry, is an uncompromising gambling city that never sleeps. Its temperament is like two sides of a coin. One side is hell and the other side is paradise. The unique gaming industry makes it attract 39 million visitors every year. At the same time, Las Vegas has a diversified cultural and entertainment industry. In addition to the bustling street scene, various cuisines, and unrestrained shopping experience, Las Vegas also has a unique urban gameplay—show! O show, David Copperfield, Le Reve-The Dream, etc., people of all ages from all walks of life can become their fans.

◎会展之都 /Capital of Convention and Exhibition

拉斯维加斯金沙会展中心、拉斯维加斯会议中心和曼德勒海湾会议中心名列全美十大会展中心。会展场地面积位列全美第三位，但经济效益排名第一。拉斯维加斯是全球会展业的黄金之地，国际汽车零部件及售后服务展（AAPEX）、国际消费类电子产品展（CES）、春秋季服装博览会等已经成为全球知名的品牌展会。每年将近 22,000 场会议在拉斯维加斯会议中心举行，包括各行业的大型贸易展会。据报道，拉斯维加斯已连续 25 年被列为全球第一大贸易会展目的地，成为名副其实的会展娱乐之都。

Las Vegas Sand Convention and Exhibition Center, Las Vegas Convention and Exhibition Center and Mandalay Bay Convention Center are among the top ten convention and exhibition centers in the United States. The area of exhibition venues ranks third in the United States, but economic benefits are the number one. Las Vegas is the golden place for the global convention and exhibition industry. The International Automotive Aftermaket Products Expo (AAPEX), International Consumer Electronics Show (CES), Spring and Autumn Clothing Expo, etc. have become world-renowned brand exhibitions. Nearly 22,000 conferences are held in the Las Vegas Convention Center each year, including large-scale trade shows in various industries. It is reported that Las Vegas has been listed as the world's largest trade exhibition destination for 25 consecutive years, becoming a veritable exhibition and entertainment capital.

◎豪华酒店汇聚 /Collection of Luxury Hotels

酒店业大亨们具有极强的前瞻性，对拉斯维加斯城市发展脉搏的把握精准，将酒店打造成多元化的旅游目的地。威尼斯人度假酒店可以在酒店中乘坐小舟体验美好的休闲时光；凯撒宫赌场度假酒店拥有"地狱厨房"主厨开设的餐厅；拉斯维加斯纽约赌场酒店可以玩过山车穿过酒店。这些独特的酒店令游客仿佛置身于威尼斯、热带雨林、瀑布和火山中。大量的顶级酒店通过新潮、极致的娱乐度假体验及高质量的服务水准和品牌格调，吸引了大量的度假型游客。

Hotel tycoons are highly forward-looking and have a precise grasp of the city development in Las Vegas, making the hotel a diversified tourist destination. Venetian Resort Hotel can experience a wonderful leisure time by boat in the hotel; Caesar Palace Casino Resort Hotel has a restaurant set up by the chef of "Hell's Kitchen"; Las Vegas New York Casino Hotel can play a roller coaster through the hotel. These unique hotels make tourists feel as if they are in Venice, tropical rain forest, waterfall, and volcano. Various top hotels attract a large number of holiday tourists through their trendy, extreme entertainment and vacation experience, as well as high-quality service standards and brand style.

参考文献

[1] 澳大利亚 Lonely Planet 公司 . 孤独星球 Lonely Planet 旅行指南系列——欧洲 [M]. 北京：中国地图出版社，2016.

[2] 澳大利亚 Lonely Planet 公司 . 孤独星球 Lonely Planet 旅行指南系列——东欧 [M]. 北京：中国地图出版社，2018.

[3] 澳大利亚 Lonely Planet 公司 . 孤独星球 Lonely Planet 旅行指南系列——IN·成都 [M]. 2 版 . 北京：中国地图出版社，2019.

[4] 澳大利亚 Lonely Planet 公司 . 孤独星球 Lonely Planet 旅行指南系列——IN·广州 [M]. 北京：中国地图出版社，2016.

[5] 澳大利亚 Lonely Planet 公司 . 孤独星球 Lonely Planet 旅行指南系列——IN·杭州 [M]. 北京：中国地图出版社，2014.

[6] 澳大利亚 Lonely Planet 公司 . 孤独星球 Lonely Planet 旅行指南系列——IN·上海 [M]. 2 版 . 北京：中国地图出版社，2017.

[7] 《亲历者》编辑部 . 深圳深度游 Follow Me [M]. 4 版 . 北京：中国铁道出版社，2020.

[8] 王洋 . 北京的走法 [M]. 北京：中国旅游出版社，2016.

[9] 魏国燊 . Explore China [M]. 北京：五洲传播出版社，2017.

[10] 宣庆坤，郭燕 . 中国人文之旅：青岛 [M]. 合肥：安徽科学技术出版社，2016.

[11] 宣庆坤，吴涛 . 中国人文之旅：北京 [M]. 合肥：安徽科学技术出版社，2016.

[12] 宣庆坤，赵子游 . 中国人文之旅：西安 [M]. 合肥：安徽科学技术出版社，2016.

[13] 宣庆坤，朱涵葆 . 中国人文之旅：厦门 [M]. 合肥：安徽科学技术出版社，2016.

[14] 朱培松 . 南京微旅行：漫游这座城 [M]. 北京：北京出版社，2018.

图书在版编目（CIP）数据

会奖目的地概况：汉英对照/ 柯淑萍主编. — 杭州：
浙江大学出版社, 2021.11
ISBN 978-7-308-21907-5

Ⅰ. ①会… Ⅱ. ①柯… Ⅲ. ①旅游地—概况—世界—
汉、英 Ⅳ. ①F590.3

中国版本图书馆CIP数据核字(2021)第220779号

会奖目的地概况（汉英对照）

柯淑萍　主编

责任编辑	李　晨
责任校对	郑成业
封面设计	春天书装
出版发行	浙江大学出版社
	（杭州市天目山路148号　邮政编码310007）
	（网址：http://www.zjupress.com）
排　　版	杭州林智广告有限公司
印　　刷	杭州高腾印务有限公司
开　　本	787mm×1092mm　　1/16
印　　张	9.25
字　　数	200千
版 印 次	2021年11月第1版　　2021年11月第1次印刷
书　　号	ISBN 978-7-308-21907-5
定　　价	36.00元